Federal Rules of Evidence
with Cues and Signals
for Good Objections

Second Edition

With 2017 Amendments

Federal Rules of Evidence with Cues and Signals for Good Objections

Second Edition

With 2017 Amendments

Deanne Siemer
Attorney at Law
Washington, DC

NATIONAL INSTITUTE FOR TRIAL ADVOCACY

Address inquiries to:
Reprint Permission
National Institute for Trial Advocacy
1685 38th Street, Suite 200
Boulder, CO 80301-2735
Phone: (800) 225-6482
Fax: (720) 890-7069
E-mail: permissions@nita.org

ISBN 978-1-60156-833-5
e-ISBN 978-1-60156-834-2
FBA 1833

Library of Congress Cataloging-in-Publication Data

Names: Siemer, Deanne C., author. | National Institute for Trial
    Advocacy
(U.S.), issuing body.

Title: Federal rules of evidence with cues and signals for good objections:
    as amended to December 1, 2018 / Deanne Siemer, Attorney at law,
    Washington, DC.

Description: Boulder, CO : National Institute for Trial Advocacy, [2018].

Identifiers: LCCN 2018029775 (print) | LCCN 2018030984 (ebook)
    | ISBN 9781601568342 (ebook) | ISBN 9781601568335

Subjects: LCSH: Evidence (Law)--United States. | United States.
    Federal Rules of Evidence. | Court rules--United States.

Classification: LCC KF8935 (ebook) | LCC KF8935 .S535 2018
    (print) | DDC 347.73/6--dc23

LC record available at https://lccn.loc.gov/2018029775

. Wolters Kluwer

Official co-publisher of NITA.
WKLegaledu.com/NITA

Contents

Introduction:
Basic Stuff—Read This

There are two really annoying things about objections: first, there are so many of them, and second, the points at which they can be made successfully come and go really quickly. A lawyer defending at a deposition or trial may be stretched to get them right. This guide gives you the "cues" to listen for as your opponent poses questions and the "signals" to look for when your opponent tries to use exhibits. These cues and signals help you recognize available objections in a timely way—which is to say as fast as possible.

What This Book Covers

Using objections successfully requires a two-step mental process. First, you have to be able to recognize that you have a good objection to the question just asked, the answer being given, or the exhibit about to be used. Second, you have to decide whether it is in your client's interest to make that objection for the record. We deal here only with the first step in applying the evidence rules in a deposition or trial—*recognizing* the objection. If you can recognize quickly that an objection is available and know that it is a good objection under the rules, then you can move efficiently to the second and urgently important step of deciding on *making* the objection. You will usually rest your decision about making the objection on very case-specific factors about the witness, the opposing lawyer, and the judge.

We use the Federal Rules of Evidence and the common law with respect to objections as applied in the federal courts. Most states have similar rules and practices.

How the Material Is Organized

More than sixty objections may apply to oral testimony and more than twenty objections may be available against exhibits. This presents a formidable task if a lawyer tries to memorize them all at once. Most people find it more useful to focus on mastering the higher priority, higher potential payoff objections first. Mastering the higher priority objections will give you the best chance at limiting your opponent to using only information that is fairly allowed under the rules. This is not, of course, to suggest that the higher priority objections on our list are always the highest priority in any deposition or trial. Sometimes objections on our lower priority list will be of utmost importance in preventing harm to your client. We say only that, in general, the objections on the higher priority list are ones that you most want to avoid missing if they are applicable to your case.

The easiest way to be truly effective in using objections is to limit the number of things you have to think about. When your opponent is presenting oral testimony, you can focus just on the objections that apply to oral testimony; when your opponent picks up an exhibit, you can shift your focus to the objections that apply to exhibits.

Part One of this book deals with objections to oral testimony.

Your higher priority list of objections starts with oral testimony because oral testimony usually makes up the large majority of the evidence you will face in the typical deposition or trial. The rules and practices with respect to oral testimony have accumulated over hundreds of years, so it is not surprising that there are so many potential objections.

Oral testimony can come at you quickly with little time to prepare for objections, so mastering the high priority objections to the content and form of questions and answers should be a primary focus. Make sure you can spot these objections and argue them to a judge without needing any reference materials.

Part Two of this book covers objections to exhibits.

By segregating objections to exhibits from the many more numerous objections to oral testimony, you keep your focus narrowed to the range of things you have to think about for what is confronting you right now—not everything in the rules book.

Most judges want objections to exhibits ruled on before trial, so ordinarily you will have time to prepare your objections and you can consult the overall checklist of objections to be sure you haven't missed anything.

Part Three of this book covers specialized objections relevant only to trials.

These are the objections to opening statements, judicial notice, presumptions, and closing arguments.

Objections to opening statements and closing arguments are risky. An adverse ruling can be given undue weight by jurors no matter what the judge instructs them on objections. But you can come prepared with your list of potential objections to glance at while your opponent speaks. On the second or third time your opponent goes over the line, your objection can be quick and concise.

Five Important General Points

First, you won't find everything in the rules. Some of the objections you will find here are grounded specifically in the federal rules and the citations are provided. Others are grounded in common law and customary practice but covered generally by Rule 611(a), which provides:

Control by court; Purposes. The court should exercise reasonable control over the mode and order of examining witnesses and presenting evidence so as to:

(1) make those procedures effective for determining the truth;

(2) avoid wasting time; and

(3) protect witnesses from harassment or undue embarrassment.

Taking testimony at depositions is made subject to this rule by Federal Rule of Civil Procedure 30(c)(1) which provides in part:

> The examination and cross-examination of a deponent proceed as they would at trial under the Federal Rules of Evidence, except Rules 103 [rulings on evidence] and 615 [excluding witnesses].

Second, the ethics rules require that you have a good-faith basis for making an objection. Rule 3.1 of the Model Rules of Professional Conduct provides:

> A lawyer shall not bring or defend a proceeding, or assert or controvert an issue therein, unless there is a basis in law and fact for doing so that is not frivolous . . . .

You cannot make objections for the sole purpose of coaching the witness, disrupting opposing counsel, suggesting the existence of facts excluded by the rules from admissibility, or unfairly influencing the fact-finder.

Third, not every good objection is worth making. Strategic judgments about your theory of the case and how you are presenting your case may mean passing up some good objections. Similarly, tactical judgments with respect to whether a point has already been established, how a particular witness is being examined, the judge's disposition toward objections at this juncture in the case, or other factors specific to your case may also mean allowing some good objections to go by.

Fourth, make your objections in a proper manner, no matter what they are. In the federal system, Rule 103(a)(1) provides:

> A party may claim error in a ruling to admit
> or exclude evidence only if [the party]. . .
> **(A)** timely objects or moves to strike; and
> **(B)** states the specific ground unless it was
> apparent from the context . . . .

Federal Rule of Civil Procedure 30(c)(2) states that in depositions:

> An objection must be stated concisely in
> a non-argumentative and non-suggestive
> manner.

Some states have rules that limit an opponent to saying "objection" and nothing more unless an opponent asks for the basis for the objection. In general, in federal court proceedings, whether at deposition or trial, you should simply say, "Objection, leading" or "Objection, hearsay." Do not say more unless the judge—or opposing counsel at a deposition—invites more discussion.

Fifth, most judges want objections to evidence resolved in pretrial proceedings, with motions in limine most often used for this purpose. This is particularly true with objections to exhibits and portions of deposition transcripts that may be used at trial. Objections to such matters during trial risk jurors misperceiving evidence when objections are sustained or overruled. Such objections also take up time.

Much of what has been written about objections assumes that most objections are made at trial. That is not so anymore—most cases are resolved before trial, and increasingly they are resolved on summary judgment or partial summary judgment motions. Evidence from deposition transcripts can be vital in pretrial motions practice.

At trial, if you don't make a timely objection, you've almost always waived it. At deposition, the rule is not quite so absolute; but in many instances, if you don't make a timely objection, you've likely waived it. And

---

that means your opponent can use the transcript as is for any purpose: to support pretrial motions, or to contradict, support, or—in some instances—substitute a witness's deposition testimony at trial. Federal Rule of Civil Procedure 32(d)(3) governs waiver as it applies to objections at depositions; the rule provides generally that if you do not object before the end of the deposition to a matter that could be cured at the deposition, then you've waived the objection. Federal Rule of Evidence 103(e) provides a general exception for when a party misses an objection and allows a court to take notice of "a plain error affecting a substantial right." But that covers very few situations where parties are represented by counsel and is usually of little comfort.

The goal here is not to teach the law of evidence. This material provides a practical way—by listening for particular cues when dealing with oral testimony or watching for specific signals when dealing with exhibits—for you to recognize when an objection is available. You can then engage the rest of the mental process you need to make strategic and tactical decisions successfully in the fast-moving context of a deposition or trial.

PART ONE:
RECOGNIZING GOOD OBJECTIONS TO ORAL TESTIMONY

Below you will see a categorized list of objections used by lawyers in dealing with oral testimony. Starting with objections to questions and answers is a practical approach because these objections generally constitute the highest volume of objections and highest pay-off situation. Because there are a great many potential objections to oral testimony, do not to try to master them all at once. There are two ways to slice this mass of objections.

Higher Priority versus Lower Priority

The higher priority objections are those experienced trial lawyers point to as protecting your client from important problems that occur with regularity in depositions and at trial. The lower priority objections are less important because they either usually don't return much of value or occur infrequently. Of course, sometimes one or more of these lower priority objections can become very important depending on the circumstances. The high versus low priority system simply gives some order to the process of mastering all these objections.

Content versus Form

If you miss objections, you can be hurt both by the content of a question and by the form of a question asked by the examiner.

Objections to content may apply either to the examining lawyer's question or the witness's answer. A bad question may bring out an unobjectionable answer. And the answer to a perfectly proper question might contain damaging and objectionable content, particularly if the witness is friendly with the examiner's side and has been coached on what important points to get across. Questions that involve improper content are generally more damaging, so by focusing on mastering content objections first, you will get better results in most cases.

Questions in an improper form can also be damaging, but some restraint in objecting to them is usually a good idea. Otherwise you risk littering the record with objections that don't really get anywhere and could result in annoying the court.

Listening to Questions

Here's an outline for listening to questions. You'll find detailed oral cues to listen for in the pages that follow.

1) Question calls for improper *content*—
   HIGHER PRIORITY

   ✓ Hearsay

   ✓ Opinion/conclusion

   ✓ Privileged communication

   ✓ Speculation

2) Question is in improper *form*—HIGHER
   PRIORITY

   ✓ Leading (on direct examination)

   ✓ Assumes facts not in evidence

   ✓ Mischaracterizes the evidence

   ✓ Misquotes the witness

3) Question lacks foundation under important
   specific rules—SPECIAL SITUATIONS

   ✓ Improper impeachment

   ✓ Improper character evidence

- ✓ Improper habit and routine evidence
- ✓ Improper refreshing recollection with a document
- ✓ Telephone call not authenticated

4) Question calls for prohibited *content*— SPECIAL SITUATIONS

- ✓ Subsequent remedial measures
- ✓ Liability insurance
- ✓ Offers of compromise, offers of payment of medical expenses
- ✓ Pleas and plea discussions

5) Question calls for improper *content*— LOWER PRIORITY

- ✓ Beyond the scope (of direct or cross)
- ✓ Calls for immaterial answer
- ✓ Calls for irrelevant answer
- ✓ Calls for a narrative answer
- ✓ Needlessly presenting cumulative evidence
- ✓ Undue delay

- ✓ Unfair prejudice (inflammatory)

- ✓ Violation of the "best evidence" rule (content of document or photo)

- ✓ Violation of parol evidence rule (terms of a contract)

- ✓ Wasting time

6) Question has an improper *form*—LOWER PRIORITY

   - ✓ Ambiguous

   - ✓ Argumentative

   - ✓ Asked and answered (repetitive)

   - ✓ Badgering the witness

   - ✓ Compound

   - ✓ Confusing

   - ✓ Embarrassing the witness unreasonably

   - ✓ Harassing the witness

   - ✓ Oppressing the witness unreasonably

   - ✓ Unintelligible

   - ✓ Vague

Listening to Answers

An examiner's question may be completely appropriate and unobjectionable, but the witness's answer may nonetheless include improper content. Witnesses have often been prepared on "important points" in the case and may rush to support those points even when the question is not directly asking for that information. The objections to the content of answers are, with a few exceptions, the same as the objections to the content called for by questions.

1) Answer includes improper *content*—
   HIGHER PRIORITY

   ✓ Hearsay

   ✓ Opinion/conclusion

   ✓ Privileged communication

   ✓ Speculation

2) Answer includes prohibited *content*—
   SPECIAL SITUATIONS

   ✓ Answer refers to subsequent remedial measures

   ✓ Answer refers to liability insurance

   ✓ Answer refers to an offer of compromise, offer of payment of medical expenses

---

✓ Answer refers to a plea or a plea discussion

3) Answer includes improper *content*—LOWER PRIORITY

- ✓ Answer is immaterial

- ✓ Answer is irrelevant

- ✓ Answer is a narrative that does not allow a fair opportunity to object

- ✓ Answer is nonresponsive to the question asked

- ✓ Answer includes improper character evidence

- ✓ Answer needlessly presents cumulative evidence

- ✓ Answer involves a telephone call not authenticated

- ✓ Undue delay

- ✓ Unfair prejudice (inflammatory)

- ✓ Violation of the "best evidence" rule (content of document or photo)

- ✓ Violation of parol evidence rule (terms of a contract)

✓ Volunteering

✓ Wasting time

✓ Witness lacks firsthand knowledge

When defending, you need to listen carefully to answers, giving the same focus to higher priority objections to content as you give to the examiner's questions.

QUESTIONS BY OPPOSING COUNSEL: GENERALLY HIGHER PRIORITY OBJECTIONS

Directing your focus on questions is the most productive way to stop improper testimony from becoming a useful part of the record. Far more objections apply to questions—or are more properly directed at questions—than apply to answers. Nailing the objection before the answer is ever out of the witness's mouth offers the best protection for your client's position.

The Content of Your Opponent's Questions: Four Important Objections

The higher priority objections to the *content* of your opponent's questions are:

- hearsay;

- opinion/conclusion;

- privileged communication;

- speculation.

A handy acronym for remembering the higher priority objections to *questions* seeking oral testimony from a lay witness is H-O-P-S (for **h**earsay, **o**pinion/conclusion, **p**rivilege, and **s**peculation). These objections are aimed at questions that seek information the rules deem inadmissible under most circumstances. This is usually the type of information that is too unreliable as a basis for a fact-finder's decision or is unfairly prejudicial.

When you object at deposition to the testimony of an opposing witness on the grounds of hearsay, lay opinion, or speculation, your opponent will still hear the witness's testimony and find out what the witness has to say. These are rarely grounds on which you can instruct a witness not to answer the question. Assuming the judge agrees with you, the objection simply ensures that this testimony in a deposition transcript will not be used against you in a pretrial motion or at trial.

At a deposition, when you object to a question put to one of your witnesses on the ground of privilege, Federal Rule of Civil Procedure 30(c)(2) allows you to instruct the witness not to answer.

At trial, when the witness is testifying and you object on any of these grounds, if the objection is sustained, the fact-finder will not hear the witness's testimony.

Objections to Hearsay

Hearsay is a higher priority objection because much of what is offered in evidence turns out to be hearsay. It also rates a higher priority because the hearsay rules are long and have some intricate parts, so mastery of this relatively higher frequency objection takes some work.

Hearsay: The Cues

Listen for the following cues for a hearsay objection.

Q: What did he/she/they say?

Q: What did you **hear** her/him/them say?

Q: What did he/she/they **tell** you?

Q: What did she/he/they **report** about that?

Q: What did **you learn**?

> [*Note:* This is often used as a way to avoid alerting an opponent to the hearsay that is coming. A witness can "learn" from personally inspecting something, but usually it is from what someone says, writes, or texts. If you object in time, your opponent will have to find a way around the hearsay rule.]

Q: **How do you know** that?

[*Note:* This is another way that experienced lawyers try to get hearsay on the record. If you object that the question calls for hearsay, then the witness must either come up with something that is not hearsay or the lawyer must move on.]

Q: What did you **understand** about that?

Q: What did she **indicate** about that?

[*Note:* Conduct intended as an assertion is hearsay even if no words are spoken.]

Q: Did she **nod**?

Q: What did she **point** to?

Hearsay: The Framework

In the federal system, the hearsay objection is governed by Rules 801–807. These hearsay rules have a lot of complicated provisions. When you are focused on oral testimony, you need to remember only a few bare essentials. Here's why—many hearsay provisions apply to exhibits, not oral testimony. As a practical matter, only about a third of the hearsay rules' parts and subparts apply to oral testimony. When you are dealing with oral testimony, don't drift off into worrying about the hearsay rules that apply to exhibits.

Hearsay is your most important objection when you are dealing with oral testimony, so it is critical to pare it down to its essentials because a good hearsay objection is one you do not want to miss. Here's how to get there in two simple steps.

1) You *have* a hearsay objection if the question calls for witness testimony about something a person said elsewhere—other than right there in the deposition or courtroom while under oath and subject to cross-examination.

   The basic rule against hearsay evidence covers all out-of-court statements and makes all hearsay inadmissible except as provided by the rules and relevant statutes. Rule 801(a) and Rule 802 in the federal system are typical hearsay general rules.

2) *But*, you *do not have* the objection if the person who made the statement is your client or an agent or employee of your client.

   For purposes of making the hearsay objection, the most important exclusion—and the objection you do *not* want to make—involves the statements of your client when used against your client. Those statements are defined by Rule 801(d)(2) as nonhearsay. If your opponent is asking a question that calls for a recounting of something your client said, it is almost always the case (and easy for your opponent to establish) that the statement is going to be used against your client. That is basically all the rule requires.

Professor Irving Younger memorably put it this way: anything your side ever said or did will be admissible so long as it has something to do with the case.

When you hear one of the hearsay cues, and your opponent is asking about something said by a person who is *not* your client, then you have a good hearsay objection. It is possible that your opponent will find an exemption (nonhearsay) or exception in the rule and be able to offer a rationale or elicit testimony from the witness to meet all of the rule's requirements. But again, she may not be able to do that, and you win.

For example, a statement *not* offered for the truth of its content is *not* hearsay. But if you make the objection in a timely way, your opponent will have to make the argument that the statement really is not being offered for the truth of its content. Making that argument in front of a jury often puzzles jurors because they equate "not offered for the truth" with "not truthful."

For another example, a prior statement made by the witness who is now testifying is *not* hearsay if the prior statement is inconsistent with the witness's current testimony and was given under penalty of perjury at a deposition or other proceeding. This definition of "nonhearsay" almost always applies to transcripts. In most courts, your opponent will need to lay a foundation showing the time, circumstances, and page number of the prior testimony; then she will need to offer the witness an opportunity to see the prior statement. Sometimes the "inconsistency" is not so clear, and your objection will be sustained.

For still another example, whether the out-of-court statement is a present sense impression; an excited utterance; or a present mental, emotional, or physical condition can be argued based on the requirements of the rules. These circumstances are highly case-specific and often not so clear. Again, the burden is on your opponent and your objection may be sustained.

If you decide to make the objection and your opponent protests, you can just say: "If you can point to an exemption or exception to the hearsay rule, please do that. This is an out-of-court statement, and it is hearsay."

To summarize, you make the hearsay rule very simple this way. If it is an out-of-court statement made by someone who is not your client, you can make a hearsay objection.

Objections to Questions that Call for Lay Opinion or Conclusion

Opinions or conclusions of a lay witness friendly to the examining lawyer are dangerous for a defender because they can be very persuasive and difficult to rebut even if based on flimsy grounds.

Lay Opinion: The Cues

Listen for the following cues for an objection to opinion evidence when a lay witness is testifying.

Q: Why did this happen?

Q: How did this happen?

Q: What did you conclude?

Q: What is your view about this?

Q: What is your belief about what happened?

Q: What is your estimate?

Q: Who was at fault?

Q: Who caused this to happen?

Lay Opinion: The Framework

The lay opinion objection is governed mainly by Rules 602 and 701. These rules require three important elements:

- first, a lay witness must have personal knowledge of the matters to which the witness testifies; *and*

- second, any opinion testimony from a lay witness must be rationally based on the witness's personal perception; *and*

- third, Rule 701 specifically disqualifies any opinion from a lay witness that is based on scientific, technical, or specialized knowledge. If a questioner wants to get into those areas, the questioner must first qualify the witness as an expert under Rule 702.

The opinions from a lay witness that are *allowed* under Rule 701 almost always fall into these common-sense categories:

1) Opinions about the physical condition of the witness or others based on personal observations—"he was sick," "I felt fine," "she is about six feet tall," "he weighed about 200 pounds," and similar conclusions.

2) Opinions about the mental condition of the witness or others based on personal observations—"she was acting crazy," or "he looked totally sane."

3) Opinions about alcoholic intoxication—"he was drunk."

4) Opinions about the relative speed of a car or other vehicle—"it was going really fast."

5) Opinions about a person's character (under Rule 405 and Rule 608, when character evidence is admissible under other provisions of the rules)—"he is a liar," or "she is a truthful person."

6) Opinions about the identity of a voice heard on a recording under Rule 901(b)(5)—"that was Sally speaking."

The rules on lay opinions envision a situation where a questioner lays a proper foundation about the personal knowledge of the witness before asking the witness for any kind of opinion. Because the foundation must come before the question seeking the witness's lay opinion, the objection may be to the lack of foundation.

When a witness is asked for a conclusion, the question may require the witness to "fill in the blanks" with respect to things the witness herself did not personally see, hear, or experience. Anything that goes beyond the personal perception by the witness is objectionable as outside the permissible limits of a lay opinion.

You can think of it this way: a lay witness provides just the news, no editorials.

Improper Expert Opinion

Objections to opinions offered by experts depend highly on the individual expert's credentials and methods and usually require considerable preparation. Here is a brief summary.

Rule 702 provides the requirements to qualify as an expert. An objection is available if you can point to any of the following factors.

- This is not an issue that scientific, technical, or other specialized knowledge will help the trier of fact understand the evidence or determine the issue.

- This witness does not have sufficient credentials in one or more of the following areas:

    - knowledge;

    - skill;

    - experience;

    - training;

    - education.

- This witness does not have sufficient facts or data.

- This witness did not use reliable principles or methods.

- This witness has not applied the relevant principles or methods reliably to the facts of the case.

Rule 703 provides a basis for the objection that the facts or data used by an expert are not of a type reasonably relied on by experts in this field in forming opinions or inferences on the subject at issue in the case.

In addition, the Supreme Court's decision in *Daubert v. Merrell Dow Pharmaceuticals*[1] provides the procedural basis for objections to expert opinions. The judge makes the threshold determination of whether the scientific knowledge the expert wants to present is valid. In doing so, the judge will consider whether the expert's methodology has been tested or subjected to scientific peer review or published in scientific journals, the rate of error involved in the technique, and general acceptance in the expert's field.

---

1. 509 U.S. 579 (1993).

Objections to Questions that Call for Privileged Communication

Privileged communications are very important for a defender. The privilege objection ensures that important lawyer-client confidences are not disclosed. The privilege can be waived if you do not make a timely objection when your client's witness is being questioned.

Privileged Communication: The Cues

Look for the following kinds of communications in the federal system.

- Attorney-client

- Doctor-patient

- Marital

- Classified national security

The following additional communications may be privileged in a case where the rule of decision is supplied by state law.

- Accountant-client

- Clergy-penitent

- Psychological counselor-client (e.g. rape or child abuse counselors)

Listen for the following cues for an objection to privileged communications.

> Q: What did **you say** (*or* **email** *or* **write**) **to your lawyer** (*or* **doctor** *or* **spouse**)?

> Q: What did **your lawyer** (*or* **doctor** *or* **spouse**) **say** (*or* **email** *or* **write**) **to you**?

> Q: How long did **you and your lawyer** (*or* **doctor** *or* **spouse**) **talk about this**?

> Q: Did **you give your lawyer** (*or* **doctor** *or* **spouse**) **any documents**?

> Q: Did **your lawyer** (*or* **doctor** *or* **spouse**) **go over any documents with you**?

> Q: **Why did you consult a lawyer** (*or* **doctor** *or* **spouse**)?

Privileged Communication: The Framework

Federal Rules of Evidence 501 and 502, which cover privilege, do not deal with the substantive law of privilege. Rule 501 defers to federal common law in federal question cases and to state law in diversity cases. Rule 502 deals only with the circumstances under which, in federal court proceedings, there is a waiver of the attorney-client privilege.

Not everything about a privileged communication is covered by the privilege. In general, for the privilege to apply, there must be a qualifying relationship, an expectation of confidentiality, and a communication made for the purpose of getting advice. Questions about any of these qualifying matters are not objectionable.

- Who was there?

- Where did the communication occur?

- When did the communication occur?

- How (by what method) did the client communicate with the lawyer?

For purposes of making objections, you should focus on the *content* of the confidential communication.

Just a note about one of the wrinkles in this area—there are two types of spousal privilege. In civil cases, the privilege operates like other privileges. In criminal cases, the privilege belongs only to the testifying spouse.

Objections to Questions that Call for Speculation

Speculation is a first cousin to an improper lay opinion. When a witness speculates about how or why something happened, as the defender, you are likely to be faced with a "dump" of unfavorable testimony. Speculation is not admissible evidence because the witness does not have firsthand knowledge. Indeed, the witness may not have any knowledge at all, just a series of thoughts about possibilities.

Speculation: The Cues

Listen for the following cues for an objection to a question that calls for the witness to speculate.

Q: Is it **possible** that . . . ?

Q: What is your **guess** about that?

Q: If you don't know the exact amount, can you give me an **estimate**?

Q: What do you **think happened** here?

Q: What is your **theory** about that?

Q: Why do you **suppose** she acted like that?

Q: What was Mr. Jones **thinking** at the time? [Speculation about what was in the mind of another person.]

Q: **What motivated** Mr. Jones to move his business to Florida?

Q: **What caused** the manager to fire Helen Stevens?

Q: **Suppose/assume** the fact was X, would that change your mind?

Q: **What if** . . . ?

Speculation: The Framework

The objection to speculation by the witness has two bases in the rules.

Rule 602 provides that a witness may not testify about a matter unless the witness has personal knowledge of the matter. Speculation is the witness's "guess" about what happened; or it is the witness's reasoning or theory based on conjecture or supposition. It is not the witness's personal knowledge of what actually happened.

Rule 701 limits testimony by a lay witness as to the witness's opinion. Speculation is often also a matter of opinion. *See* discussion of the objection to lay opinion above.

Objecting to speculation can be very important because it can prevent the witness from dumping into the record all the witness's ideas, positions, impressions, thoughts, suppositions, and reasons about some issue at hand.

The Form of Your Opponent's Questions: Four Important Objections

The higher priority objections to the *form* of questions asked by your opponent are:

- leading on direct examination;
- assumes facts not in evidence;
- mischaracterizes evidence;
- misquotes the witness.

An easy acronym for remembering these objections is L-A-M-M. The acronym just reminds you to be on the lookout for these potential objections. These objections are directed at ways of phrasing a question that under most circumstances are not suitable for obtaining useful information in a fair way.

Objections to Leading Questions (On Direct)

Leading questions suggest the answer. They basically involve the lawyer testifying and the witness confirming the lawyer's propositions. This objection has a higher priority because of the frequency of leading questions in witness examinations, particularly at depositions.

Leading Questions: The Cues

Listen for the following cues for an objection to a leading question.

First, any question on direct examination is likely leading if it **does *not* begin with** the traditional key words.

- Who
- What
- Where
- When
- Why
- How
- Describe
- Explain

Second, a question on direct examination is likely leading if it has a factual predicate and **ends with** one of the following phrases.

- ". . . isn't that right?"
- ". . . that's correct, isn't it?"
- ". . . didn't you?"
- ". . . wasn't it?"

Third, a question may be leading if it suggests to the witness the desired answer and **calls for a "yes" or "no" answer** from the witness. Some favorite forms of these questions begin with the following.

- "So, [*reciting facts*] . . . ."
- "Therefore, [*reciting facts*] . . . ."

Leading Questions: The Framework

Here's the simple way to think about it: you can object to leading questions on direct examination if one of the following two things is true.

- When counsel for your opponent is questioning one of *your opponent's own witnesses*; or

- When counsel for your opponent is questioning *a third-party witness* who is not identified with your client (and therefore not identified with an adverse party).

Don't use the "leading" objection when opposing counsel is questioning *your client's witnesses* if your client is a party to the action.

In the federal system, Rule 611(c) governs the use of leading questions. In general, it does not allow leading questions on direct examination.

There are three exceptions where leading questions are allowed on direct examination:

- The first is when a party calls an adverse party or a witness identified with an adverse party. Your opponent can always ask leading questions of an adverse party or witness.

- The second is when a party calls a hostile witness. Before asking leading questions about the case, your opponent must establish hostility first. This is usually done by showing the witness's bias, interest in the outcome of the case, or generally uncooperative manner.

- The third exception is when a leading question is necessary to develop the witness' testimony. This usually means

  - Questions phrased to follow the exact wording of an evidence rule when laying a proper foundation;

- Or questions to orient the witness to the time and place about which the questioner wants to question the witness;

- Also questions about background information, such as the witness's education or employment; or about preliminary matters that are not directly at issue;

- The exception also covers questions to a witness who is a child, who is disabled, or someone who otherwise might have difficulty in communicating well.

Objections to Questions that Assume Facts Not in Evidence

There are four kinds of questions that mislead the witness and all are objectionable. They fall under the general heading of "assumes facts not in evidence." A question may misquote a witness's prior testimony; mischaracterize, misstate, or improperly describe the evidence in the case; or even present facts not in evidence in the case at all.

Questions that Assume Facts Not in Evidence: The Cues

Listen for the following cues for an objection to this kind of question.

Misquotes the witness's prior testimony.

- Q: Just a short while ago **I heard you say** that . . . [*when the witness has said something different*].

- Q: Didn't **you just say** that . . . .

- Q: **You previously testified** that . . . .

- Q: **You told** the police officer/investigator that. . . .

Mischaracterizes the prior evidence.

Q: Mary Smith **said in her testimony** that the weather was cold, so my question to you is. . . [*when Mary did not say that*].

Q: Exhibit 12 **says on its face** that Mr. Jones was in charge of this matter, so how is it that . . . [*when Exhibit 12 is subject to several interpretations*].

Q: The **evidence in this case shows** that the toxic waste was on the east side, so I want to ask you . . . [*when the evidence points mostly to the south*].

Improperly describes prior evidence.

Q: We have some **very powerful evidence** in this case about how long it took the ambulance to get to the scene. What were you doing during that time?

Q: The **convincing evidence** of misconduct in this case . . . .

Q: The very tenuous evidence of payment . . . .

Assumes facts not in evidence at all.

Q: **We all know that** . . . .

Q: **It is a fact that** . . . .

Q: **It must have been** . . . .

Questions that Assume Facts Not in Evidence: The Framework

None of the federal rules specifically provide for this objection. A court would sustain this kind of objection under the general authority in Rule 611(a).

Rule 611(c), which prohibits leading questions, offers a related basis. Questions that fall into this category are sometimes classified as one type of "leading" questions because they are "misleading" questions.

Rule 602 also offers a related basis:

> A witness may testify to a matter only if evidence is introduced sufficient to support a finding that the witness has personal knowledge of the matter.

Just listening to a lawyer's presentation of facts in a question would not, by itself, qualify a witness to testify about those facts. (The lawyer's recitation of facts in a question on direct examination is also likely leading the witness.)

The ethics rules may also apply in this situation. Model Rule of Professional Conduct 4.1(a) provides that in the course of representing a client, a lawyer shall not knowingly make a false statement of material fact or law to a third person; and Rule 3.4(e) provides that in trial, a lawyer shall not allude to any matter that the lawyer does not reasonably believe is relevant or that will not be supported by admissible evidence.

Asking questions that assume facts not in evidence can be one of the most pernicious ways of examining a lay witness. No matter how well prepared, most lay witnesses are not experienced enough at parsing questions to look hard at the factual predicate for a question from an opposing lawyer. You would need to object to point out the factual flaw in the question.

Lack of Special Foundation Required by the Rules: Five Available Objections

Most oral testimony requires a minimal foundation. First, the witness must have firsthand knowledge of the matter about which he is testifying. And second, the matter must be relevant—that is, it must have any tendency to make a fact at issue in the case more probable or less probable. These foundation requirements are almost always readily established.

In a few cases, however, your opponent will need additional foundation required by the evidence rules before asking a question about particular subject matter. If she has not laid the required foundation before she asks the question, then you have an objection available.

These objections apply to:

- evidence about telephone calls;

- habit and routine evidence;

- character evidence;

- obtaining evidence by refreshing recollection with a document; and

- evidence used for impeachment of a witness.

One way to deal with these objections for specialized situations—other than trying to memorize them—is to have a summary of the requirements of the rules on a sheet of paper in a standard plastic sheet protector that goes with you to every deposition or trial.

Objections to Questions that Lack Foundation for the Content of Telephone Conversations

You may have an objection based on the lack of foundation for a telephone call or sound recording if the call or recording is not authenticated before the witness testifies about its content.

The Cues

Listen for the following cues:

> Q: Tell us about the **telephone conversation** you had with . . . .

> Q: In the **phone call** with Sally, did you . . . ?

> Q: When you **phoned** (*or* **called** *or* **buzzed** *or* **rang up**) . . . .

The internet equivalents are also covered.

> Q: When you **Skyped** with . . . .

> Q: When you got on **Google Chat** with . . . .

> Q: When you connected on **FaceTime** with . . . .

> Q: When you used the **Internet phone service** with . . . .

> Q: When you signed on to the **videoconference** (*or* **audioconference**) with . . . .

Telephone Call or Voice Recording: The Framework

Rule 901(b)(5) recognizes one common way to lay a foundation with respect to the identification of a voice on a phone call through testimony that the witness is familiar with the voice and recognized it. Specifically,

1) that the witness heard the voice

2) at some prior time or occasion in the past

3) under circumstances connecting the voice with the alleged speaker.

Rule 901(b)(6) covers authentication of telephone conversations where the call was made by the witness by evidence that a call was made to the number assigned at the time by the telephone company to a particular person or business; and

- *[for a call to a person]* either self-identification (by the person who answered the call) or circumstances that show the person answering the call to be the person who was called.

- *[for a call to a business]* the call was made to the place of business and the conversation related to business reasonably transacted over the telephone.

Objections to Questions that Lack Foundation for Habit and Routine Evidence

Your opponent may try to prove that a particular action was taken by proving habit and routine with respect to taking that action.

The Cues

Listen for these kind of things.

> Q: Is it your **habit** to . . . ?
>
> Q: What is the **custom** of your department . . . ?
>
> Q: Is it your assistant's **usual practice** to . . . ?
>
> Q: Did you follow your **routine (or routine practice)** on August 10 . . . ?
>
> Q: What is the **standard way** your division processes . . . ?
>
> Q: What is the **conventional way** you would tackle a problem like this?
>
> Q: Is there a **tradition** for when this happens?
>
> Q: What is the **pattern** that usually occurs?

Improper Habit and Routine Evidence: The Framework

Rule 406 governs objections to evidence of a personal habit or the routine practice of a business or other organization. This kind of evidence is allowed as circumstantial evidence that on the specific occasion at issue in the case, the person or organization acted in a way consistent with the personal habit or routine practice. The objection rests on the failure to prove the elements of foundation, which are:

- personal knowledge of the witness; and

- a sufficient number of instances of the specific prior conduct that allow the court to qualify the conduct at issue as a habit or routine.

The rule on habit and routine is permissive in that it allows this evidence regardless of whether there were eyewitnesses to the actual event in question and regardless of whether the testimony about habit or routine is corroborated.

Objections to Questions that Lack Foundation for Character Evidence

The objections to character evidence usually arise when opposing counsel wants to prove that a person has in the past acted consistently with his or her established character and therefore likely acted in the same way on a specific occasion.

The Cues

Listen for

- Questions about a person's particular character trait, suggesting that therefore the person has a propensity to act in a **particular** way.

- Questions about a person's particular character trait, suggesting **no propensity** to act in a particular way.

Improper Character Evidence: The Framework

Rule 405 provides that when character is admissible it can be proved by reputation, opinion, or specific acts. Character is admissible, for example, when it is an essential element of a claim or defense, such as a libel case in which a person claims his character has been defamed. These rules usually apply only to criminal cases where the accused puts at issue his own character or the character of the victim.

Rule 404(a) bars character evidence when character is used to show a propensity to act in accordance with character. The idea is that if you are going to introduce evidence to prove character—and then use that character to prove some issue material to the case—that chain of inference is barred. Thus, a disputed fact cannot be proved by reputation, opinion, or specific acts.

In arguing objections to character evidence, one area of difficulty is that habit may be admissible under Rule 406 to prove that a person acted in a particular way on numerous instances in the past and therefore acted the same way on a specific occasion. But character is not admissible under Rule 404 to do essentially the same thing.

One way to think about this is that character is a general disposition that can be shown by behavior in a variety of ways. For example, honesty can manifest itself in many different ways. Habit, on the other hand, is a more specific disposition that manifests itself by behavior in a narrow way. For example, chain smoking manifests itself only with respect to smoking.

Most jurisdictions have special rules on character evidence in sexual assault and child molestation cases. In the federal system, Rules 412, 413, 414, and 415 establish special exceptions in which specific prior acts can be proved to establish a propensity to commit the acts at issue in the case.

Objections to Questions that Lack Foundation for Refreshing the Witness's Recollection

Occasionally your opponent may have a witness who forgets some important fact while testifying. This can happen because the witness is tired or stressed; or it can happen for less benign reasons. Your opponent may want to show the witness a document to refresh the witness's recollection about that fact. To do that, your opponent will have to lay a specific foundation.

The Cues

The scenario with respect to refreshing recollection with a document usually goes like this:

> Q: I want to ask you now about where you were on March 3.

> A: Well, I think that was the time I was on vacation in Barcelona, but I don't really remember the exact dates right now.

> Q: Well, I show you your diary entry for March 3. Does that refresh your recollection?

This is *improper* refreshing recollection. Counsel has not followed the necessary procedure, and you have an objection available to make sure opposing counsel cannot use the document at this point.

Listen for the following other cues for this objection:

Q: Perhaps we can **refresh your recollection** on that.

Q: Would it **help you to remember** if I showed you X?

Q: This **document might help you remember.**

Q: Here is a **document that you might remember about that**. Let me ask you to look at that.

Improper Refreshing Recollection: The Framework

Refreshing recollection is generally a matter of common law. In most jurisdictions, refreshing recollection can only be done if a proper foundation is laid. So your objection will rest on the absence of an adequate foundation. You will be listening carefully to see if your opponent does it this way without missing any of the steps:

1) The examiner asks about a fact relevant to an issue in the case.

2) The witness testifies that he or she now does not have a full or partial memory about the facts sought.

---

3) The examiner marks a document containing refreshing memory information for identification and shows it to opposing counsel.

4) The examiner then shows the document to the witness asks the witness to read the document to himself.

5) The witness silently reads the portion of the document that relates to the question asked. Unless there is an independent foundation for the document, the refreshing document cannot be read aloud by the witness and the refreshing document cannot be admitted into evidence.

6) The examiner asks whether reading the document refreshes the witness's recollection about the fact she asked about initially.

7) The witness testifies that his memory has been refreshed by looking at the document.

8) The examiner takes the document from the witness (so the witness is now testifying from his memory and not from the document).

9) The examiner asks the same question about the fact relevant to an issue in the case.

10) The witness answers from the refreshed recollection.

In the federal system, Rule 612 refers to the situation where a lawyer is refreshing a witness's recollection with a document. The rule presumes such refreshing recollection is appropriate under common law and specifies protections for the adversary. The document used to refresh the witness's recollection must be made available to opposing counsel at the hearing and before cross-examination.

Objections to Questions that Lack Foundation for Impeachment

The last in this category of things that require a particular foundation is impeachment. The common law and the rules attempt to contain the kinds of evidence that can be used to impeach a witness because this can easily get off into areas of little relevance or utility to the issues in the case.

Improper impeachment can occur either when a witness's credibility is challenged in cross-examination of that witness or when a separate character witness has been called to testify about a previous witness's credibility.

The Cues

Look for the following situations.

- Your opponent cross-examines a witness by asking about specific bad acts *other than* those bearing on a character of untruthfulness.

- Your opponent asks a witness about crimes other than convictions (Rule 609).

- Your opponent asks a witness about convictions for misdemeanors (imprisonment for less than one year) (Rule 609(a)(1)).

- Your opponent asks a witness about convictions that occurred more than ten years ago (Rule 609(b)).

- Your opponent asks a witness questions seeking to impeach with evidence of religious beliefs (Rule 610).

- Your opponent calls a character witness and asks about specific bad acts of a prior witness (whose testimony is being impeached) rather than by opinion about reputation or character.

- Your opponent calls a character witness and asks about the reputation in the community of a prior witness (whose testimony is being impeached) for character *other than* untruthfulness.

- Your opponent calls a character witness and asks that witness about his opinion of the character of a prior witness (whose testimony is being impeached) for character *other than* untruthfulness.

You have a good objection when any of these questions are asked.

Improper Impeachment: The Framework

In general, when your opponent starts on a line of questions about bad acts or bad character of a witness important to your case, an objection to improper impeachment will help keep the inquiry within fair limits. It will force your opponent to put the line of questions under one of the methods of proper impeachment.

To defend your objection, you need to be able to articulate what is *proper* impeachment and why your opponent cannot fit within those limits.

Under common law, your opponent is entitled to question the witness about:

- memory (lack of memory or impaired ability to remember);

- perception (which is an impaired ability to perceive due to the time, place, and circumstances when the witness claims to have perceived relevant information);

- bias (which is a predisposition in favor not based on admissible evidence);

- prejudice (which is a predisposition against not based on admissible evidence);

- interest (a stake in the outcome of the case); or

- corruption (bribery for the testimony being given).

Any witness can be impeached using one of these traditional methods. In the federal system, Rule 607 provides for impeachment of any witness by any party, including the party calling the witness.

In addition, there are three more methods of *proper* impeachment, but these are subject to some limitations:

- prior inconsistent statement;

- character or reputation for untruthfulness;

- conviction of certain crimes.

Rule 613 allows impeachment with the witness's *prior inconsistent statement* as long as the witness has been given an opportunity to explain or deny the statement.

Rule 608 allows impeachment with respect to a witness's *character or reputation for untruthfulness* in two ways.

- First, the witness who is currently testifying can be impeached by cross-examining the witness about specific bad acts that illustrate the witness's character for untruthfulness,

- but *not* about any other kinds of bad acts.

- Second, a character witness can be called to attack a prior witness's character for truthfulness by direct examination about reputation in the community for untruthfulness or by opinion about the prior witness's character for untruthfulness,

- but *not* about specific bad acts of the prior witness, and

- *not* about any aspects of the character of the prior witness *other than* for untruthfulness

Rule 803(21) provides an exception to the hearsay rule for statements concerning a person's reputation in the community concerning character.

Rule 609(a)(2) allows impeachment with evidence of a *conviction of any crime involving a dishonest act or false statement* that occurred within the last ten years.

Subject Matter Prohibited by the Rules: Four Automatic Objections

The rules provide four situations in which particular content is off limits for examining counsel. These rules are aimed at fairness. They exclude certain content because, for social policy reasons, this kind of evidence has no place in the proof of a claim or defense. They are:

- subsequent remedial measures;

- liability insurance;

- offers of compromise or offers to pay medical expenses; and

- pleas and plea discussions.

Some lawyers think of these as the "automatic objection" subjects, meaning that when you hear one of these subjects mentioned you would "automatically" have a good objection. In fact, the rules on each of these include very limited exceptions under which testimony on these subject matters can be allowed. However, your automatic objection will force your opponent to identify the exception provided by the rule (e.g., Rule 411 on Liability Insurance: "such as proving a witness's bias or prejudice or proving agency, ownership, or control.").

At deposition, the witness will testify about these matters regardless of a pending objection because these are not subjects on which the rules allow you to instruct the witness not to answer. But your objection will prevent the transcript portions containing this testimony from being used in pretrial motions or at trial (if the judge concurs, of course).

These excluded subject matters may bring the good-faith-basis rule into play. Model Rule of Professional Conduct 3.1 provides:

> A lawyer shall not bring or defend a proceeding, or assert or controvert an issue therein, unless there is a basis in law and fact for doing so that is not frivolous . . . .

The objection that there is no good faith basis for asking a question—one that mentions liability insurance, for instance—forces your opponent to state the facts or sources of information on which he is relying to support the contention that one of the exceptions is available.

One way to keep in mind the areas covered by these rules is the acronym S-L-O-P (for subsequent remedial measures, liability insurance, offers of compromise, and pleas). The S-L-O-P rules are in Article IV of the Federal Rules of Evidence, which is entitled "Relevance and its Limits," so some commentators describe the S-L-O-P subjects as "not relevant." The S-L-O-P rules also come after Rule 403, which deals with unfair prejudice, so you can think of them as "legislated unfair prejudice." In any case, if the question calls for information about one of these subjects, an objection is available.

The S-L-O-P rules are subject to the general common law "opening the door" rule, under which a party's actions may lead the court to admit evidence the rules otherwise would make irrelevant or inadmissible. The underlying idea is that there may be a need to cure any disadvantage that one party may have gained by offering the testimony that "opened the door." Therefore, if some testimony in your case has "opened the door," you may have lost your objection when your opponent begins questioning about one of these subject matters.

Objections to Questions about Subsequent Remedial Measures

Subsequent remedial measures are actions that, if taken prior to the injury or harm at issue in the case, would have made that injury or harm less likely to occur. Remember that this objection covers only measures "subsequent" to or after the event that gave rise to the cause of action.

Subsequent Remedial Measures: The Cues

Listen for the following cues for an objection to this kind of question.

> Q: Was anything **fixed after** the accident?
>
> Q: What **changes were made to your procedures** after the complaint was filed?
>
> Q: What **measures did you take later to prevent** this from happening again?
>
> Q: Did you **do things differently after** this problem occurred?

Subsequent Remedial Measures: The Framework

Rule 407 governs the objection to evidence about subsequent remedial measures.

Under this rule, evidence would not be admissible to prove:

- negligence;
- culpable conduct;
- a defect in a product;
- a defect in a product's design;
- a need for a warning or instruction.

However, there are some exceptions—such evidence can be admitted to prove the following, if any are controverted issues in the case:

- ownership, if disputed;
- control, if disputed;
- feasibility of precautionary measures, if disputed.

You can also use this evidence to impeach a witness.

Objections to Questions about Liability Insurance

Liability insurance protects the insured from the risks of *liabilities* created by lawsuits and similar claims. It covers the insured in the event they are sued for claims that come within the coverage of the policy. The objection does not apply to other forms of insurance.

Liability Insurance: The Cues

Listen for the following cues for an objection to this kind of question.

Q: [*Any mention of* "insurance" *or* "coverage" *or* "policy."]

Q: What did **you pay out of your own pocket** as a result of this problem?

Q: As far as **cash payments that you yourself made**, in what amount were you damaged?

Q: **Who paid** for your expert witness (*or* videos *or* illustrative exhibits)?

Liability Insurance: The Framework

Rule 411 governs objections to testimony about liability insurance. It covers evidence that a person was or was not insured against liability.

Such evidence is not admissible to prove:

- whether a person acted negligently; or

- whether a person acted wrongfully.

However, such evidence can be admitted to prove:

- agency;

- ownership;

- control;

- bias or prejudice of a witness who is being paid by an insurance carrier.

Objections to Questions about Offers of Compromise or Offers to Pay Medical Expenses

The federal rules, and most state rules or statutes, protect persons who offer to settle claims from having those offers used against them at trial.

Offers of Compromise: The Cues

Listen for the following cues for an objection to this kind of question.

> Q: Tell us **everything you said to the plaintiff,** Mr. Jones, right after the accident.

> Q: You didn't want the plaintiff, Mr. Jones, **to have to pay for these medical expenses,** did you?

> Q: You expected there would be a **settlement** (*or* **agreement** *or* **way of avoiding a trial**) in this matter, isn't that right?

Offers of Compromise: The Framework

Rule 408 governs the objection to evidence about compromise, and Rule 409 governs the objection to evidence about payment of medical expenses. These rules cover evidence of furnishing, promising, offering, or accepting compromise or medical expenses.

Such evidence is not admissible to prove (under circumstances where the claim is disputed):

- liability for a claim;

- invalidity of a claim;

- amount of a claim.

Additionally, this evidence may not be used to impeach a witness through prior inconsistent statement.

Rule 408 offers a very limited exception: "when offered in a criminal case and when the negotiations related to a claim by a public office in the exercise of its regulatory, investigative, or enforcement authority." Rule 409 on medical expenses provides no exceptions.

Objections to Questions about Pleas and Plea Discussions

Statements made by a person who made a plea to a criminal charge or was a participant in plea discussions generally cannot be used against that person at trial.

Pleas and Plea Discussions: The Cues

Listen for the following cues for an objection to this kind of question:

> Q: You remember once being involved in a crime?

> Q: You have said to the police in the past that . . . ?

Pleas and Plea Discussions: The Framework

Rule 410 governs the objection to pleas and plea discussions. Such statements are not admissible to prove:

- a plea later withdrawn;

- a plea of nolo contendere;

- any statements made in plea discussions.

However, there are some exceptions—such statements can be admitted:

- when another statement made in the course of the same plea or plea discussions has been introduced ("opening the door");

- in a criminal proceeding for perjury if the statement was made under oath.

This rule is basically the criminal evidence equivalent of Rule 408 on compromise and offers of compromise on the civil side. It protects only the person accused in the criminal proceeding in which the plea or plea discussions were had, and the rule applies in both civil and criminal cases.

QUESTIONS BY OPPOSING COUNSEL: GENERALLY LOWER PRIORITY OBJECTIONS

The evidence rules and hundreds of years of common-law practice provide many objections to the content of a question beyond those in the "higher priority," "lack of foundation," and "special situation" categories discussed above. These objections are of lower priority because either they don't often produce useful results or they don't often arise.

The Content of Your Opponent's Questions: Seven Lower Priority Objections

The following objections are directed to the *content* sought by the question:

- beyond the scope (of direct or cross);

- calls for an immaterial answer;

- calls for an irrelevant answer (fails Rule 402 test of relevance);

- calls for a narrative answer;

- needlessly presents cumulative evidence;

- will cause undue delay;

- will create unfair prejudice;

- violates the "best evidence" rule (content of document or photo);

- violates the "parol evidence" rule (written contracts);

- wastes time.

There are, of course, occasions when one of these lower priority objections becomes highly important because of the special circumstances of a particular case. Classifying these objections as "lower priority" is an effort to give some guidance on the learning process with respect to the very numerous objections that can apply to oral testimony.

Objections to Questions that Are Beyond the Scope of Direct or Cross-Examination

The objective of cross-examination after direct, or re-direct after cross, is to deal with the subject matter raised by the opponent in the immediately prior examination. New subject matter must await a different witness.

Beyond the Scope: The Cues

Listen for the following cues for an objection to "beyond the scope."

- **New subject matter**, other than questions directed at the credibility of the witness.

- **New person** mentioned in a question.

Beyond the Scope: The Framework

Rule 611(b) provides that cross-examination should not go beyond the subject matter of direct examination. Most judges follow an informal corollary to that rule and do not allow re-direct examination to go beyond the subject matter of the prior cross-examination.

The rule creates an exception to the no-new-subject-matter requirement—a witness's credibility is always a legitimate subject of cross-examination. Credibility usually encompasses two kinds of inquiries:

- whether the witness has the capacity to testify accurately and fully:

    - perception;

    - memory;

    - clarity;

- and whether the witness has any motive *not* to testify accurately and fully:

    - bias;

    - prejudice;

    - interest in the outcome of the case;

    - corruption.

The rule also gives judges considerable leeway in this area. At trial, the court may allow questioning beyond the scope of the preceding direct or cross-examination, but the cross-examiner must proceed "as if on direct examination" (Rule 611(b)). This generally means that leading questions will not be allowed.

Objections to Questions that Call for Irrelevant or Immaterial Answers

The concepts of relevance and materiality basically require litigants to stick to the issues in the case.

Irrelevant or Immaterial: The Cues

Listen for the following cues for an objection to a question that calls for an "irrelevant" or "immaterial" answer.

- The information sought **does not make any difference in determining a fact** that is "of consequence" in the case (*relevance*).

- The information sought **does not relate to an issue** in the case (*materiality*).

Only two elements are necessary for an adequate foundation for most oral testimony: 1) the witness has firsthand knowledge; and 2) the testimony is relevant to a fact at issue in the case. The objection can be either "irrelevant" or "no foundation."

Irrelevant or Immaterial: The Framework

Rule 401 defines relevance broadly to include evidence that has

- any tendency

- to make a fact more or less probable

- than it would be without the evidence

- and the fact is of consequence in determining the action.

Rule 402 provides that evidence that is not relevant is not admissible.

To meet an objection on relevance grounds, the proponent of the evidence must first point to a fact that is of consequence in determining an issue in the case and then show the evidence being offered has some (however small) tendency to make the existence of that fact more or less probable.

There is no rule that covers the concept of materiality. In general, materiality looks to the issues that are pleaded in the case. If the evidence sought to be admitted relates to an issue that has been removed from the case (perhaps by stipulation) or that has not been pleaded, then you can block it with an objection to materiality.

Many commentators assume that "relevance" and "materiality" cover about the same ground.

Objections to Questions that Call for Narrative Answers

A question that calls for a narrative answer is one that asks the witness in essence to "tell a story" or make a broad-based and unspecific response. The problem is that it is too general, allowing the witness to "narrate" a series of occurrences—any of which may produce hearsay, opinion, be irrelevant, or otherwise constitute inadmissible testimony.

Narrative Answers: The Cues

Listen for the following cues for an objection to a question that calls for a narrative answer.

> Q: Tell us **everything you know** about . . . .
>
> Q: What is **your complete recollection** about . . . ?
>
> Q: Tell me **in your own words how** this happened.
>
> Q: Explain **everything you observed** on this occasion.
>
> Q: Please tell us **all the conversations you had** with Mr. Jones.

Narrative Answers: The Framework

There is no specific federal rule on this subject. The general terms of Rule 611(a) allow a court to sustain objections to questions that call for a narrative answer.

This objection is used primarily at trial. It is based on the difficulty that this kind of question poses for the defender, whose ability to make specific objections to the content being offered by an opposing counsel's question may be seriously impaired. The witness's story or narrative may include inadmissible material that is in front of the jury before the defender has an opportunity to keep the material out.

Objections to Questions that Lead to Needless Cumulative Evidence, Undue Delay, or Wasting Time

These are related objections that have to do with efficiency during trial. With oral testimony, cumulative evidence usually takes the form of testimony by a number of different witnesses about the same fact without adding anything new. In a jury trial, repeating the same fact over and over again can give an unfair emphasis to that fact, while diminishing other equally important facts.

Needless Cumulative Evidence: The Cues

Look for:

- testimony from a witness on subjects or exhibits that the witness has already gone over more than once;

- testimony from additional witnesses that only repeats testimony previously given without adding any factual information;

- additional testimony offered on a point already sufficiently established;

- corroborating evidence on a point that has already been corroborated;

- unnecessary testimony on a point no longer in issue—perhaps by stipulation, response to a request for admissions during the discovery process, judicial notice, or presumption.

Needless Cumulative Evidence: The Framework

Rule 403 provides that relevant evidence may be excluded if its probative value is substantially outweighed by a danger of undue delay, wasting time, or needlessly presenting cumulative evidence.

Cumulative evidence is allowed. The rule is aimed at essentially repetitive evidence that does not bring any new information to the determination of the action.

Objections to Questions that Involve Unfair Prejudice

"Unfair prejudice" usually refers to evidence that would have an undue tendency to cause a juror to use an improper basis when deciding an issue—and that basis is commonly, though not necessarily, an emotional one.

Unfair Prejudice: The Cues

Look for pretrial opportunities to challenge oral testimony that will create an adverse impression of the witness without central relevance to the issues in the case:

- **moral character,** such as excessive drinking, gambling, drug use, sexual activity;

- **physical violence,** such as fighting, beatings, child abuse;

- **gruesome testimony,** such as verbal descriptions of oozing wounds, severed body parts, or dead bodies.

Unfair Prejudice: The Framework

Rule 403 provides that relevant evidence may be excluded if its probative value is substantially outweighed by a danger of unfair prejudice.

This is an objection used primarily at trial. Inflammatory testimony may arouse emotions—such as sympathy, disgust, anger, or revulsion—to such an extent that the testimony disrupts the jurors' rational processes of consideration of the evidence. You should usually deal with matters of unfair prejudice by pretrial motions in limine.

Objections to Questions that Violate the "Best Evidence" Rule

The "best evidence" rule is a common-law principle that to prove the content of a document or photograph, the best evidence is the original of the document or photograph itself.

"Best Evidence" Rule: The Cues

Listen for the following cues for an objection based on the "best evidence" rule.

> Q: What was in the **written notice** that you received? [*Before a foundation has been laid for the notice.*]

> Q: What does the **video** (or **photograph**) **show**? [Before a foundation has been laid for the video or photo.]

> Q: What was **contained in her letter**? [Before a foundation has been laid for the letter.]

"Best Evidence" Rule: The Framework

Rule 1002 requires that to prove the content of a writing, recording, or photograph, the original writing, recording, or photograph is required. Under Rule 1003, a duplicate of the writing, recording, or photograph is sufficient.

In general, the objection as it applies to oral testimony is that testimony about the content of a writing, recording, or photograph is not the "best evidence" and that the writing, recording, or photograph has to be produced unless there is an adequate reason why it cannot be produced.

In any case, the witness may testify about certain facts about a document, recording, or photograph:

- that it exists;
- that it was signed;
- that it was delivered in a certain way.

These circumstances are not the "content" of the exhibit as that term is used by Rule 1002.

In addition, you don't have to qualify a photograph if a witness testifies about what she personally saw— which is what is depicted in that photograph. And under Rule 1004(d), a witness may testify about the content of a writing, recording, or photograph if that content is "not closely related to a controlling issue."

If the writing, recording, or photograph is not available because it has been lost, destroyed, or is unobtainable, then under Rule 1004, "other evidence" of its contents is admissible. Oral testimony is included in such "other evidence," and there is no hierarchy of "other evidence."

Objections to Questions that Violate the Parol Evidence Rule

The parol evidence rule is a common law doctrine to the effect that no forms of extrinsic evidence, such as oral testimony, are admissible to prove the terms and conditions of a written contract. Only the contract itself can be used for that purpose.

Parol Evidence Rule: The Cues

Listen for the following cues for an objection based on the parol evidence rule.

> Q: **Prior to the time you entered the contract** with Ms. Smith, **what discussions did you** have with her about the contract?

> Q: **What did you tell** Ms. Smith about what you wanted in the contract?

> Q: **At the time you were negotiating this contract, what did you understand the term** "insured" **in the contract meant**?

Parol Evidence Rule: The Framework

No federal rule sets out the parol evidence rule. Rather, federal courts and most state courts follow this common-law rule that applies only to contracts.

The parol evidence rule applies primarily to evidence of discussions or negotiations prior to or contemporaneous with the completion of the contract.

THE FORM OF YOUR OPPONENT'S QUESTIONS: FIVE LOWER PRIORITY OBJECTIONS

Lower priority objections directed to the *form* of an opponent's questions may include anything on this list:

- ambiguous;

- argumentative;

- asked and answered (repetitive);

- badgering;

- compound;

- confusing;

- embarrassing;

- harassing;

- oppressing;

- unintelligible;

- vague.

For purposes of making these objections, similar or overlapping concepts are usually combined into the five objections explained below.

Many of these objections, no matter how they are named, have to do with the personal style of your opponent, and your inclination to use these objections will be influenced by whether anything important is going on. As with other "lower priority" objections, circumstances may arise that make these objections urgently necessary.

With respect to depositions, Federal Rule of Civil Procedure 30(d)(3) provides:

> At any time during a deposition, the deponent or a party may move to terminate or limit it on the ground that it is being conducted in bad faith or in a manner that unreasonably annoys, embarrasses, or oppresses the deponent or a party.

One important consideration here is that you should always have a good-faith basis for making an objection. Making an objection just to alert the witness to pay particular attention—such as the objections to ambiguous, asked and answered, confusing, unintelligible and vague—is not always appropriate. Rule 30(d)(2) provides:

> The court may impose an appropriate sanction—including reasonable expenses and attorney's fees incurred by any party—on a person who impedes, delays, or frustrates the fair examination of the deponent.

These objections describe questions that occur with reasonable frequency, particularly in depositions. But making a lot of these objections may produce a record that annoys the court. For example, a federal district court judge sanctioned a partner in one of the largest national law firms for making these kinds of objections to excess.

> [I]n preparation for a hard-fought product liability jury trial, I was called upon by the parties to rule on numerous objections to deposition transcripts that the parties intended to use at trial. I noticed that the deposition transcripts were littered with what I perceived to be meritless objections made by one of the defendant's lawyers . . . . I was shocked by what I read. Thus, for the reasons discussed below, I find that Counsel's deposition conduct warrants sanctions.
>
> * * *
>
> In defending depositions related to this case, Counsel proliferated hundreds of unnecessary objections and interruptions during the examiner's questioning. Most of these objections completely lacked merit and often ended up influencing how the witnesses responded to questions. In particular, Counsel engaged in three broad

categories of improper conduct. First, Counsel interposed an astounding number of "form" objections, many of which stated no recognized basis for objection. Second, Counsel repeatedly objected and interjected in ways that coached the witness to give a particular answer or to unnecessarily quibble with the examiner. Finally, Counsel excessively interrupted depositions that Counsel defended, frustrating and delaying the fair examination of witnesses.[2]

---

2. *Security National Bank of Sioux City, Iowa v. Abbott Laboratories*, Case 5:11-cv-04017-MWB (N.D. Iowa July 28, 2014), pp. 4, 10.

Objections to Questions that Are Ambiguous, Confusing, Unintelligible, Vague

These objections are all directed at questions posed in a manner that confuses the witness so the answer to the question may not reflect true information.

Confusing the Witness: The Cues

These types of questions have some general characteristics:

- questions that do not direct the witness to something demonstrably at issue in the case:

  - **no date, place, or time specified** so the witness's answer could apply to any date, place, or time;

- questions prefaced by terms as to which there may be no common understanding or meaning:

  - in general;

  - fundamentally;

  - basically;

  - normally;

  - on average;

  - usually;

  - ordinarily;

  - commonly;

so that while the witness may have one meaning in mind, the questioner or court or jurors may have another meaning in mind.

Confusing the Witness: The Framework

No federal rule covers these forms of questions specifically. However, Rule 611(a) directs the court to "exercise reasonable control over the mode . . . of examining witnesses . . . so as to make those procedures effective for determining truth."

Rule 403 provides that relevant evidence can be excluded if its probative value is substantially outweighed by a danger of confusing the issues or misleading the jury.

Questions in these categories are either susceptible to differing interpretations or so nonspecific as to invite the witness to wander into areas that may be objectionable. However, the usual follow-up to this kind of objection is for examining counsel (at a deposition) or the judge (at trial) to ask the witness whether the witness understands the question. If the witness says "yes," then the objection doesn't work. Judges are sometimes wary of this kind of objection because the objection may be interposed only to warn the witness to be careful in answering and not because there is really anything wrong with the question.

Objections to Questions that Are Argumentative

These are questions that make counsel's argument to the fact-finder by the way the question is phrased.

Argumentative: The Cues

Look for questions that include:

- counsel's summary of the witness's prior testimony;

- counsel's comment on the evidence;

- counsel's inferences drawn from the evidence.

Q: **In light of your testimony that** you were tired that night, how can you now say that . . . ?

Q: **Given that you've already admitted** you could hardly see because of the snow, why do you think that . . . ?

Argumentative: The Framework

No federal rule specifically covers these questions. Rule 611(a) is the general authority for the objection.

This objection generally does not apply to situations where the examiner is arguing with the witness.

The objection to that type of question is usually badgering, harassing, or embarrassing the witness (*see* discussion below on those objections). The "argument" in the question, rather, is directed at the fact-finder in an attempt to persuade. When the examining lawyer poses this kind of question, she may not care about the witness's answer at all. She makes her point with the question.

Objections to Questions that Have Been Asked and Answered

These are repetitive questions usually seeking to develop some inconsistency in the witness's testimony.

Asked and Answered: The Cues

This objection is available when

- the **same question** has been asked;

- by the **same counsel;**

- and calls for the **same testimony** the witness has already given.

Asked and Answered: The Framework

Rule 403 allows exclusion of relevant evidence "if its probative value is substantially outweighed by a danger of . . . needlessly presenting cumulative evidence." When the same question is asked by the same examiner again and again, this is usually needless cumulative evidence. Rule 611(a) is also available as a basis for this objection.

This objection is not available when different counsel asks the question. For example, the witness is asked the question on direct and then again on cross. However, the objection would be available if examining counsel asks the question on direct and the same examining counsel asks the question again on re-direct.

Objections to Questions that Are Badgering, Harassing, Unreasonably Embarrassing, Oppressing the Witness

These objections, all mentioned in rules and evidence texts, are basically directed at forms of harassing a witness unfairly.

Harassing the Witness: The Cues

Examining counsel is badgering and harassing a witness when she:

- **mocks** a witness;

- tries to **antagonize or provoke** a witness;

- does **not give a witness an opportunity** to finish an answer to a question;

- makes **derisive comments** about the witness or asks derisive questions (e.g., "You expect anyone to believe that?");

- uses an unnecessarily **hostile, harsh, or combative manner** in asking questions;

- unreasonably quarrels with, shouts at, or threatens **a witness**.

Examining counsel is embarrassing or oppressing a witness when she:

- asks about **humiliating, shaming, distressing, or disconcerting** conduct not closely related to the issues in the case;

- asks about **immigration status or other law enforcement matters** not related to the issues in the case or the character of the witness.

Harassing the Witness: The Framework

Rule 611(a)(3) provides that the court may "protect witnesses from harassment or undue embarrassment." Federal Rule of Civil Procedure 30(d)(3) allows a motion to limit or terminate a deposition "on the ground that it is being conducted in . . . a manner that unreasonably annoys, embarrasses, or oppresses the deponent or party."

On occasion, these tactics—badgering, harassing, and oppressing—go beyond the wording of questions to the witness. They may also include actions by counsel (usually at a deposition where counsel is out of sight of a judge) such as using a very loud voice, standing or leaning over the witness, refusing to give the witness a break until the witness finishes answering a long series of questions, providing no water, using uncomfortable furniture, placing a witness in the glare of sunlight through a window, and the like.

Objections to Compound Questions

Compound questions essentially ask two or more questions in one, such as did you do X and Y — so that a single answer could be true as to one part of the question and not true as to another part.

Compound Questions: The Cues

Listen for the following cues for an objection to this kind of question.

- The word "**and**" between two parts of a question:

  Q: How satisfied are you with your job **and** your commute?

  Q: When John gave you the document **and** Sarah lifted the cover of the box, what happened next?

  Q: What was his reaction **and** next step?

- The word "**or**" between two parts of a question:

  Q: Where did this happen **or** where were you at the time?

  Q: What did you do **or** exactly how did you get there?

- The word "**still**" or "**instead**" indicating two sets of conditions:

    Q: Are you **still** angry with Sam? [two questions here: "Were you angry with Sam before now?" and "Are you angry with Sam now?"]

    Q: **Instead** of opening all these envelopes, did you give some to Sam?" [two questions here: "Did you open all the envelopes?" and "Did you give some of the envelopes to Sam?"]

Compound Questions: The Framework

No rule governs compound questions directly. Rule 611 provides the general framework.

A compound question has two or more distinct parts or asks for two or more items of information together. That can make it either difficult or impossible to get a clear meaning from the witness's answer. The objection essentially asks that the various parts be disaggregated so that the witness can answer the questions separately and each of the answers will be clear.

Compound questions are also difficult for the witness if they suggest that there are only two alternatives: "Did you do [this] or [that]?" In fact, the witness may have done something other than what the questioner is assuming. Compound questions are often confusing to a lay witness who may answer one part of the question and forget to go back to the other part. This kind of question on direct examination is also usually leading the witness.

Compound questions should be relatively easy to cure, but if they are allowed to stand, the record may be significantly less useful. Whether that is a consideration in deciding to make the objection is one governed by your strategy and tactics in the case, a subject not covered here.

WITNESS ANSWERS TO YOUR OPPONENT'S QUESTIONS

Occasionally an unobjectionable question will be responded to by an objectionable answer from the witness. The objections to witnesses' answers fall into the same high priority/low priority categories applied to counsel's questions.

In addition, you may have an objection when a witness's answer is not responsive to the question asked or when the witness volunteers information that was not called for by counsel's question.

Answers: Higher Priority Objections

If the question is proper as to content and form, then listen carefully to the answer given by the witness to spot the higher priority objections, which are the same as those for questions.

- Is the witness testifying to hearsay (even though the question did not call for hearsay)?

- Is the witness giving his opinion or conclusion that goes beyond the kinds of common-sense opinions or conclusions as to which lay persons are permitted to testify?

- Is the witness talking about a privileged conversation with his lawyer (even though the witness has been warned not to)?

- Has the witness lapsed from facts the witness knows through firsthand knowledge into speculation about what the witness supposes happened, has an idea about, predicts, philosophizes, or thinks might be the case.

The considerations with respect to making these four **high priority** objections to answers are the same as for making those objections to questions. They are described in the section above on objections to the content of questions. Answers that include hearsay, lay opinion, or speculation are especially dangerous because they can include material that is not legally relevant and is highly prejudicial. This can be hurtful to your client's cause if you do not stop it with a timely objection.

Answers: Lower Priority Objections

An objection to an answer interferes with the way the witness wants to relate what she knows, so use this kind of objection sparingly. There are certainly times when an objection is required to protect important rights, but those do not occur often.

In objecting to a witness's answer that comes after a proper question—or that sometimes comes after an improper question that suggests the answer the questioner wants—you have available all of the lower priority "content" objections:

- answer is irrelevant or immaterial;

- answer is improper character evidence;

- answer involves a telephone call not authenticated;

- answer is a narrative that does not allow fair opportunity to object;

- answer is nonresponsive to the question asked;

- answer is speculation;

- answer needlessly presents cumulative evidence;

- answer refers to excluded subject matter (subsequent remedial measures, liability insurance, offers of compromise, pleas and plea discussions);

- undue delay;

- unfair prejudice;

- violation of the "best evidence" rule (content of document or photo);

- violation of the "parol evidence" rule (written contracts);

- wasting time;

- volunteering;

- witness lacks firsthand knowledge.

The considerations that go into making most of these objections to are the same as for making those objections to questions. They are described in the sections above on lower priority objections to the content of questions.

The following are the issues you should consider with respect to objections to a nonresponsive answer or to an answer that volunteers information not called for by the question.

Objections to Nonresponsive Answers

Nonresponsive answers may happen when a witness is not paying attention and misses the point of a question. More often, this happens when a witness is ducking a hard question.

Nonresponsive Answer: The Cues

Listen for the following cues for an objection to this kind of question.

- The witness's answer **fails to respond to the question** posed by the examiner.

- The witness responds with **information that does not answer the question**.

Nonresponsive Answer: The Framework

No federal rule covers this objection. The objection is grounded in the common-law principle that the examining counsel is entitled to require a witness to respond to a fair question.

Technically, the objection belongs to the questioner. This problem usually occurs on cross-examination (although it can also occur on direct, particularly of a hostile witness). And technically, the examiner's response is a motion to strike the nonresponsive answer. However, judges often allow an objection to a nonresponsive answer from defending counsel so that the problem can be cleared up quickly.

Objections to Answers with Volunteered Information

"Volunteering" is a general term for testimony given by a witness that doesn't have much to do with the question asked. This sometimes occurs when a witness has been coached that certain testimony is helpful to the case, so the witness looks for a place to make that point.

Volunteered Answer: The Cue

Listen for the following signal for an objection to this kind of question.

- The answer **exceeds the scope of the ques-tion**.

Volunteered Answer: The Framework

No federal rule covers this objection. The objection is grounded in the common-law principle that the witness can be required to limit an answer to the fair response to the question posed.

The objection usually belongs to the questioner. This problem sometimes occurs on cross-examination (although it can also occur on direct, particularly of a hostile witness).

When you are defending, your objection to an answer that exceeds the scope of the question needs to be on specific substantive grounds, such as relevance, prejudice, hearsay, lay witness opinion, or similar grounds. The theory is that unless there is a substantive basis to object to the answer, the witness's volunteered answer is not a matter of concern to an opposing lawyer.

The objection is typically accompanied by a motion to strike the "volunteered" information.

PART TWO: RECOGNIZING GOOD OBJECTIONS TO EXHIBITS

You have available many powerful objections you can use when dealing with exhibits—four potential objections to the foundation for an exhibit, and more than twenty potential objections to the content of an exhibit. You can also use almost all of these objections to exclude oral testimony, and how to do so has been covered in Part One. In some cases, however, objections apply differently for exhibits. The task is to spot an available objection quickly and efficiently.

We deal here with objections to all types of exhibits—documents, physical objects and substances, photographs and medical images, audio and video recordings, animations, and models. The objections may apply to some types of exhibits and not others, but when they do apply, the objections and the underlying rationale are almost always the same.

When defending, objections to exhibits are easier to deal with than objections to oral testimony. The content of an objectionable document, for example, usually contains easy-to-spot signals that will you lead you to the applicable objection. In most cases, you will have the advantage of discovery. You will have a chance to scrutinize most exhibits, especially document exhibits, in your office and take your time noting potential objections. If you scan the discovery documents into digital format, a digital search capability makes identifying potential objections even easier. You can search the whole document collection for the various signals to the potential objections and then look carefully at the documents the search turns up.

Using a two-part framework helps makes this process more efficient. In general, you will want to look first at the foundation for the exhibit. That is often your strongest objection. Second, consider the content of the exhibit for possible objections. You can group this fairly large number of content objections into higher and lower priority to give some order to the process of considering these objections.

Remember that when defending, you also have available many of the objections to the form of a question that seeks either to introduce or obtain information from the witness about an exhibit. Those objections to the form of the question are covered in detail in Part One on oral testimony and that material is not repeated here.

THE FOUNDATION FOR YOUR OPPONENT'S EXHIBITS: OBJECTIONS TO LACK OF FOUNDATION

The objection to foundation, if it is available, is usually the defender's strongest objection to an exhibit. It is also one of the easiest to master because, in the federal system and most state systems, it involves only four rules—Rule 602 on personal knowledge, Rule 401 on relevance, and Rules 901 and 902 on authentication, all of which are basically uncomplicated.

The first thing to know about objections to foundation for exhibits is that Rule 902 basically waives the need to establish a foundation for exhibits within any of twelve categories of documents, so do *not* object to the foundation for any of these:

- public document bearing a government seal;

- public document or public record that is certified;

- notarized document;

- certified document;

- official government publication;

- newspaper;

- periodical;

- labels, signs, or tags affixed in the course of a business;

- commercial paper (certificate of deposit, short-term debt instrument issued by a corporation, money market security, etc.);

- certain foreign public documents;

- certified records generated electronically;

- certified data copied from an electronic device or storage medium.

Questions of genuineness generally go to the weight of the evidence, not its admissibility.

For all other exhibits, the proponent must establish four elements of the foundation:

- "competency" of the witness to testify about the exhibit—which requires firsthand knowledge about the exhibit;

- identification of the exhibit by a description sufficient to show what it purports to be and to distinguish it from all other exhibits in the case;

- relevance of the exhibit to establishing a fact of consequence to determining an issue in the case;

- authentication of the exhibit to establish that the exhibit really is what it purports to be.

Listen carefully to be sure all four elements are there—otherwise you have a good objection to lack of foundation. A convenient acronym to keep track of these four elements for purposes of considering an objection to foundation is C-I-R-A (for **c**ompetency, **i**dentification, **r**elevance, and **a**uthentication).

These foundation requirements apply to all kinds of exhibits—documents, photographs, video and audio recordings, models, and animations. The foundation is the gateway for an exhibit, and if an objection closes that gate, you do not have to deal with the more complicated objections to the content of the exhibit, such as hearsay or the original document rules.

Objections to the Competency of the Witness

A lay witness must have personal knowledge of the matter about which the witness is testifying.

Witness Lacks Firsthand Knowledge: The Signals

Look for the following signals for an objection based on lack of personal knowledge.

- The exhibit *is not* something that the witness **personally**

    - wrote;

    - created;

    - directed the writing or creation of;

    - saw created;

    - received;

    - obtained.

- The exhibit *does not depict* something that the witness **personally**

    - saw;

    - heard;

    - smelled;

- tasted;

- had a tactile contact with, like touching, rubbing, scratching;

- acted on.

Witness Lacks Firsthand Knowledge: The Framework

Rule 602 requires that a lay witness must have "personal knowledge of the matter" about which the witness is testifying.

The Advisory Committee notes point out that the rule requires a witness who testifies about a fact that can be perceived by the senses to not only have had an opportunity to observe, but must also have actually observed the fact about which the witness is testifying.

The basic idea is to separate testimony about something that the witness knows firsthand from something the witness knows only secondhand (like hearsay) or something the witness has good reason to believe, but can only assume is true.

Objections to the Identification of the Exhibit

The identification of an exhibit is a statement as to what the proponent of the exhibit claims it to be. It is a description sufficient to distinguish the exhibit from all other exhibits in the case.

Identification: The Signal

Listen for the following question that is a signal your opponent is about to get to the identification of an exhibit.

> Q: I show you what has been marked as Exhibit 12 and ask if you can identify it.

The answer to this basic question, asked about nearly every exhibit sponsored by a witness, must satisfy the requirement for an adequate description of what the exhibit is, based on the witness's personal knowledge about the exhibit.

If opposing counsel does not ask this question and the witness starts to testify about the content or nature of the exhibit, you have an appropriate objection to lack of foundation.

Identification: The Framework

Article IX of the Federal Rules of Evidence is entitled "Authentication and Identification," and the two terms are discussed together.

Technically, the identification of an exhibit is what the proponent of the exhibit *claims* it to be. The authentication of the exhibit is evidence sufficient to show that the exhibit *really is* what the proponent claims it to be. In some cases, different witnesses must provide the identification of the exhibit and its authentication. Be aware that witnesses sometimes try to testify about the content of a document in an effort to identify it.

For purposes of making sound objections, it is a good idea to separate identification from authentication. The rules provide specific guidance on what is acceptable authentication, and to have a sound basis for using a particular method of authentication, the exhibit must first be identified so that its authentication can be measured against the proper part of these rules.

Objections to the Relevance or Materiality of the Exhibit

Relevance and materiality in exhibits are the same concepts as applied to oral testimony. The exhibit has to have something to do with the issues in the case.

Irrelevant or Immaterial: The Signals

Look at the content of the exhibit for these signals for an objection to "irrelevant" or "immaterial."

- The exhibit **does not make any difference in determining a fact** that is "of consequence" in the case (*relevance*).

- The exhibit **does not relate to an issue** in the case (*materiality*).

Irrelevant or Immaterial: The Framework

Rule 401 defines relevance broadly to include evidence that has

- any tendency

- to make a fact more or less probable

- than it would be without the evidence

- and the fact is of consequence in determining the action.

Rule 402 provides that evidence that is not relevant is not admissible.

The objection on relevance grounds calls on the proponent of the evidence to point to a disputed fact and show how the evidence being offered has any tendency to make the existence of that fact more or less probable.

There is no rule that covers the concept of materiality. In general, materiality looks to the issues that are pleaded in the case. If the exhibit sought to be admitted relates to an issue that has been removed from the case (perhaps by stipulation) or that has not been pleaded, then it can be blocked by an objection to materiality.

Many commentators assume that "relevance" and "materiality" cover about the same ground.

Objections to the Authentication of the Exhibit

Authentication is evidence sufficient to support a finding that the item is what the proponent claims it is.

Authentication: The Signals

An exhibit requires testimony to authenticate it if it falls within one of the following categories:

- document prepared or signed by someone other than the witness;

- computer printout;

- downloaded document;

- email;

- e-discovery document;

- object marked by someone other than the witness;

- sample of a substance;

- photograph or image;

- video or audio recording;

- model;

- animation.

Listen for these usual questions that signal what is coming is the testimony that will try to authenticate the exhibit.

> Q: With respect to what has been marked as Exhibit 12, how do you know . . . ?

> Q: What basis do you have for your understanding that Exhibit 12 is . . . ?

> Q: What role did you have in the preparation of Exhibit 12?

Authentication is usually the most difficult aspect of establishing the foundation for an exhibit and the most fruitful focus for an objection.

Authentication: The Framework

Rule 901 lists ten methods your opponent may try to use to authenticate an exhibit, including the testimony of a witness with knowledge, distinctive characteristics of the item, and evidence describing a process or system and showing that it produces an accurate result. Any of these may be lacking—the witness may not have sufficient firsthand knowledge, the characteristics of the item may not be distinctive enough, the evidence about a process or system may not be sufficient to show that it produces an accurate result. However, in making an objection, the usual formulation is "no foundation" without specifying what aspect is lacking.

The requirements for authentication are often confused with the exceptions to the hearsay rule because some of the categories (described in the rules governing each of these) are similar. However, authentication is a part of foundation, and hearsay is better treated separately as an objection to content as discussed below.

The Content of Your Opponent's Exhibits: Objections that Challenge Fairness

The objections to the content of an exhibit logically should come after an adequate foundation has been laid for the exhibit. Objections to foundation challenge whether the exhibit really is what the proponent says it is and has something to do with the issues in the case. Objections to content challenge the fairness in using the exhibit as evidence in deciding the case.

To deal effectively with the objections to the content of exhibits, separate them by priority and master the higher priority objections first. Raising available higher priority objections at deposition or in trial likely will do the most to advance your client's cause.

The general principles of most objections to the content of exhibits are the same as apply to the content of oral testimony. Those explanations are set out in Part One on oral testimony and are not repeated in this section on exhibit.

Content of Exhibits: Four Generally Higher Priority Objections

The higher priority objections to the content of an exhibit are those that either arise frequently or have an important payoff. They are:

- hearsay;

- opinion/conclusion/speculation;

- privileged communications;

- prior statement of a witness, improper use.

Objections to Hearsay

Every piece of paper with words written on it is a potential hearsay problem for your opponent. There are only a few guidelines to remember in making hearsay objections.

Hearsay: The Signals

Look for the following types of exhibits:

- text documents;

- sketches made by a person;

- soundtracks of voices on a video;

- audio recordings.

Exhibits that fall into each of these categories are statements a person did "not make while testifying at the current trial or hearing" (Rule 801(c)(2)) and, in the first instance, qualify as hearsay.

Everything else is probably *not* hearsay, including animations, charts, computer data printouts, diagrams, drawings, graphs, maps, medical images, models, photographs, physical objects, substances, tables, and timelines.

Hearsay: The Framework

The hearsay objection is governed by Rules 801–807. These hearsay rules have a lot of complicated provisions. However, when you are focused on exhibits, you need to remember only three things.

1) Consider a hearsay objection to every exhibit that is an ordinary text document **with two exceptions**:

    Documents created by your client.

    Do *not* make the objection if the person who wrote or created the document is **your client** or an employee or agent of your client. For purposes of making the hearsay objection, the most important exclusion, and the objection you do *not* want to make, involves the statements of your client when used against your client. Those statements are defined by Rule 801(d)(2) as nonhearsay. If your opponent is asking about your client's document, it is almost always the case (and easy for your opponent to establish) that the statement is going to be used against your client. That is basically all the rule requires.

Printed material from some public source.

Do *not* make the objection if the exhibit is some **printed matter** issued by a government, newspaper, publisher (books, magazines), or trade organization (market reports, directories). Rules 803(8)–(23) cover these kinds of exhibits.

2) Transcripts are out-of-court statements, *but* they are defined by Rule 801(d) as *not hearsay* when they are used for one of three purposes:

- to cross-examine a witness with a prior inconsistent statement;

- to rehabilitate a witness whose credibility has been attacked; or

- to identify a person as someone the declarant perceived earlier.

3) Affidavits are hearsay, just like any other out-of-court statement, *unless* an affidavit is being used for a preliminary matter. Rule 104(a) defines preliminary questions

as "whether a witness is qualified, a privilege exists, or evidence is admissible" and provides that in these cases "the court is not bound by evidence rules, except those on privilege." This means that an affidavit can be used to establish a part of the foundation for or support for an objection to an exhibit without regard to the hearsay rules.

As the defender, you don't need to worry about all the exemptions and exceptions to the hearsay rule. Only academics are interested in most of these. Go instead to the strategy and tactical considerations about *whether* to make the objection. The objection puts the burden on the proponent of the exhibit to put it within an exemption (nonhearsay) or exception. Most of these require specific elements of proof. Your objection just puts it to your opponent to supply that proof.

For example, a document *not* offered for the truth of its content is *not* hearsay. This definition of "nonhearsay" usually applies to notices, contracts, and wills. But if you make the hearsay objection in a timely way, your opponent will have to state a supportable basis for the proposition that the statement really is not being offered for the truth of its content. Otherwise, your objection will be successful.

For another example, whether a document (that is not one of your client's records) is a business record

---

can be argued based on the requirements of the rules. If you are in a deposition, it can be argued later in motion papers. If you are at trial, your opponent will have to come up with testimony from the witness that puts the statement within the rule (while you are listening to see if they get every one of the rule's requirements).

Other examples of hearsay exceptions where the rules make your opponent jump through very specific hoops are medical records (Rule 803(4)) and past recollection recorded (Rule 803(5)).

Remember that with text documents, there is often an objection to hearsay within hearsay. That is, the document itself is an out-of-court statement, and in addition, the document reports other out-of-court statements. Under Rule 805, you can object to both layers of hearsay. The proponent of the exhibit has to have an exemption or exception for the document and a separate one for the statement contained in the document.

Hearsay is an important objection when you are dealing with text documents and recordings. So it is critical to pare it down to its essentials because a good hearsay objection is one you do not want to miss.

Objections to Opinion, Conclusion, or Speculation

Documents written by lay persons often contain their opinions, conclusions, or speculations as to events or persons. Written opinions are objectionable just as oral testimony containing such opinions would be objectionable. Most judges will require redaction of lay opinions if a timely objection is made.

Opinion, Conclusion, or Speculation: The Signals

Look for the following types of exhibits:

- text documents;
- video recordings;
- audio recordings.

Then look for the following signals within the content.

- Someone's explanation of **why this happened**.

- What the person speaking on the audio or video or writing the document **concluded** about something at issue in the case.

- An expression of the author's **view about** . . . .

- The author's **belief about** . . . .

- What the author **thinks happened** here.

- A statement of the author's **estimate of** . . . .

- Someone's assessment of who was **at fault**.

- A statement about who **caused** this to happen.

Opinion, Conclusion, or Speculation: The Framework

The lay opinion objection is governed mainly by Rules 602 and 701. These rules impose three important limitations, which are the bases for an objection to a lay opinion.

- First, a lay witness must have personal knowledge of the matters about which the witness writes.

- Second, any opinion written by a lay witness must be rationally based on the witness's personal perception.

- Third, Rule 701 specifically disqualifies any opinion from a lay witness that is based on scientific, technical, or specialized knowledge. If a document or recording contains an opinion in those areas, the person who spoke the words or wrote the text must first be qualified as an expert under Rule 702.

The opinions from a lay witness that are *allowed* under Rule 701 almost always fall into one of the following categories.

1) Opinions about the physical condition of the witness or others based on personal observations—"he was sick at the time," "she is about six feet tall," "he weighed about 200 pounds," and similar conclusions.

2) Opinions about the mental condition of the witness or others based on personal observations—"she was acting crazy," or "he looked totally sane."

3) Opinions about alcoholic intoxication—"he was drunk."

4) Opinions about the relative speed of a car or other vehicle—"it was going really fast."

5) Opinions about a person's character under Rule 405 and Rule 608, when character evidence is admissible under other provisions of the rules—"he is a liar," or "she is a truthful person."

Objections Based on Privilege

The law of privilege most commonly applies to exhibits in what are known as "claw-back" occasions. These occur when there has been an inadvertent discovery production that included one or more privileged communications. Under defined circumstances, the owner of the document is entitled to "claw" it back from the party to whom it was produced.

Privileged Communication: The Signals

Look for the following types of exhibits:

- text documents;

- video recordings (such as deposition or trial preparation).

In the federal system, look for these kinds of communications:

- attorney-client;

- doctor-patient;

- marital (spouse-spouse).

And possibly these additional communications in a case where the rule of decision is supplied by state law:

- accountant-client;

- clergy-penitent;

- psychological counselor-client (e.g., rape or child abuse counselors).

Only counsel for the holder of the privilege can make the objection.

Privileged Communication: The Framework

In the federal system, Rules 501 and 502, which cover privilege, do not deal with the substantive law of privilege. Rule 501 defers to federal common law in federal question cases and state law in diversity cases.

When you as the defender make an objection to an exhibit that contains privileged communications, Rule 502 is important when it is unclear whether the attorney-client privilege has been waived.

Because a privileged communication must be one that is made with the expectation that it will be kept confidential, the disclosure of the privileged information to a third person (who is not a party to the privileged relationship, such as the attorney-client relationship) generally waives the privilege.

Under Rule 502, however, even if a document containing privileged information is turned over in discovery, and thus disclosed to third persons, this disclosure does not operate as a waiver if three conditions are met:

- the disclosure was inadvertent;

- the holder of the privilege took reasonable steps to protect from disclosure;

- the holder of the privilege took reasonable steps to rectify the error.

If these conditions are met, then the objection to disclosure of the privileged communication should succeed despite the prior disclosure and loss of confidentiality.

Objections to Prior Statement of a Witness

This objection applies primarily to the use of transcripts at trial, although prior transcripts are sometimes also used in depositions.

Prior Statement of a Witness: The Signals

Look for the following types of exhibits:

- text documents;

- video and audio recordings.

An exhibit that contains a prior statement of a witness *is objectionable* if the following is true.

- On direct examination or cross-examination of a witness, opposing counsel uses a prior statement *of a party* and *does not establish* that

    - the prior statement is offered against the opposing party; and

    - the statement was made by the party or is one the party manifested that it adopted and believed to be true.

- On cross-examination of a witness, opposing counsel uses a prior statement *of the witness* to impeach the witness's current testimony and *does not establish* that

    - the prior statement is inconsistent with current testimony;

- the prior statement was testimony given under oath; and

- the prior statement has been disclosed to counsel on the other side.

- On direct examination of a witness, opposing counsel uses a prior statement of the witness *to confirm* the witness's testimony.

Note that:

- prior consistent statements can be used only on rebuttal; and

- only after the witness has been impeached for recent fabrication or recent improper motive in testifying.

Prior Statement of a Witness: The Framework

Rule 801(d)(1)(A) exempts from the hearsay rule (and thus allows the use of) prior inconsistent statements in transcripts. The statement must have been "given under penalty of perjury at a trial, hearing, or other proceeding or in a deposition."

Rule 801(d)(1)(C) exempts from the hearsay rule (and thus allows the use of) evidence of the identification of a person. This usually applies only in criminal cases and has to do with written or video or audio reports of lineups or other identifications.

Rule 613(a) requires that if the statement is included in a document, that document must be shown to the adverse party's lawyer.

Rule 613(b) applies to extrinsic evidence of a witness's prior inconsistent statements—usually the testimony of another witness and usually applicable to oral testimony.

Content of Exhibits: Four Objections to Content Prohibited by the Rules

Some objections to exhibits have to do with special kinds of subject matter content. They are the same prohibited content that applies to oral testimony and is discussed in Part One. You will recognize them readily as the issues in the case are analyzed, so you likely will be ready for these objections from your general preparation of the case. They are:

- subsequent remedial measures;

- liability insurance;

- offers of compromise and offers to pay medical expenses;

- pleas and plea discussions.

Each of these objections is summarized below.

Objections to Subsequent Remedial Measures

Subsequent Remedial Measures: The Signals

Look for the following types of exhibits:

- text documents;

- photographs;

- video recordings.

Then look for the following signals in the content of an exhibit:

- anything that was **fixed after** the accident at issue;

- any changes that were made to procedures after the complaint was filed;

- any **measures taken later to prevent** something from happening again;

- ways of doing things differently after the problem occurred.

Subsequent Remedial Measures: The Framework

Rule 407 governs the objection to evidence about subsequent remedial measures. It covers measures that if taken prior to the injury or harm at issue in the case would have made that injury or harm less likely to occur. (Remember that the rule covers only measures "subsequent" to or after the event that gave rise to the cause of action.)

Such evidence is not admissible to prove:

- negligence;

- culpable conduct;

- a defect in a product;

- a defect in a product's design;

- a need for a warning or instruction.

There are, however, exceptions—such evidence can be admitted to prove the following, if any are controverted issues in the case:

- ownership;

- control;

- feasibility of precautionary measures.

Such evidence can also be used for impeachment purposes.

Objections to Liability Insurance

Liability Insurance: The Signals

Look for the following types of exhibits:

- text documents;
- charts;
- graphs.

Then look for the following signals in the content of an exhibit:

- references to **insurance policies**;
- any mention of "**insurance**" or "**coverage**" or "**policy**";
- information about what someone **paid out of her own pocket** as a result of the problem.

Liability Insurance: The Framework

Rule 411 governs objections to testimony about liability insurance. It covers evidence that a person was or was not insured against liability.

Such evidence is not admissible to prove

- whether a person acted negligently;
- whether a person acted wrongfully.

However, such evidence can be admitted to prove the following, if contested in the action:

- agency;

- ownership;

- control;

- bias or prejudice of a witness who is being paid by an insurance carrier.

Objections to Offers of Compromise, Offers to Pay Medical Expenses

Offers of Compromise: The Signals

Look for the following type of exhibits:

- text documents;
- video or audio recordings.

Look for the following signals in the content of an exhibit:

- **settlement** or **settle**;
- **compromise**;
- **way of avoiding litigation**.

If documents have been scanned into digital format, run a search to find possibilities.

Offers of Compromise: The Framework

Rule 408 governs the objection to evidence about compromise. Rule 409 governs the objection to evidence about payment of medical expenses. These rules cover evidence of furnishing, promising, offering, or accepting compromise or medical expenses.

Such evidence is not admissible to prove (under circumstances where the claim is disputed):

- liability for a claim;

- invalidity of a claim;

- amount of a claim;

- impeachment through prior inconsistent statement.

Rule 408 offers a very limited exception: "when offered in a criminal case and when the negotiations related to a claim by a public office in the exercise of its regulatory, investigative, or enforcement authority." Rule 409 on medical expenses provides no exceptions.

Objections to Pleas and Plea Discussions
Pleas and Plea Discussions: The Signals

Look for the following types of exhibits:

- text documents;
- video and audio recordings.

Look for the following signals for an objection to this kind of exhibit:

- plea agreements;
- correspondence about plea agreements;
- documents or recordings reflecting plea discussions.

Pleas and Plea Discussions: The Framework

Rule 410 governs the objection to pleas and plea discussions. It covers statements made by the defendant who made a plea or was a participant in plea discussions.

Such evidence is not admissible to prove:

- a plea later withdrawn;
- a plea of nolo contendere;
- any statements made in plea discussions.

However, such evidence can be admitted to prove:

- when another statement made in the course of the same plea or plea discussions has been introduced ("opening the door");

- in a criminal proceeding for perjury, if the statement was made under oath.

This rule is basically the criminal evidence equivalent of Rule 408 on compromise and offers of compromise on the civil side. It protects only the person accused in the criminal proceeding in which the plea or plea discussions were had, and the rule applies in both civil and criminal cases.

Content of Exhibits: Nine Generally Lower Priority Objections to the Content of Exhibits

Some of the terminology we use for the less central objections overlaps—certain names for objections are common in one part of the country but not in others. This section collects all the recognized names for objections in alphabetical order and, in some instances, consolidates similar concepts.

The lower priority objections to content arise less frequently or usually produce less value. They are:

- character evidence, improper;

- completeness;

- confusing;

- cumulative evidence, needless;

- misleading;

- original document requirements;

- parol evidence;

- summary of voluminous material, requirements;

- surprise;

- undue delay;

- unfair prejudice;

- wasting time.

Objections to Character Evidence
Improper Character Evidence: The Signals

Look for the following types of exhibits:

- text documents;
- recordings.

Look (or do a digital search) for the following signals of character evidence. They are references to a person's character traits:

- careful;
- dishonest;
- honest;
- industrious;
- loyal;
- peaceful;
- truthful;
- untruthful;
- violent.

They can also refer to:

- specific "bad acts" such as crimes or wrongs;
- specific "good acts" such as charity or volunteer work.

You can object to documents relating to character traits other than truthfulness or untruthfulness. Only documentary evidence related to truthfulness or untruthfulness may be used. No documents with respect to other aspects of character are admissible.

You can also object to documents displaying character traits through specific acts. Only documentary evidence of a reputation for truthfulness or untruthfulness or documents expressing someone's opinion about a witness's truthfulness or untruthfulness may be used. Even if specific acts deal with untruthfulness, they are not admissible under Rule 608(b) unless the court makes a specific ruling.

Improper Character Evidence: The Framework

The character evidence rules apply mainly to text documents, although occasionally they may apply to video or sound recordings. For a defender, the rules are useful primarily in excluding documents or recordings that comment favorably on the character of a witness on your opponent's side of the case or adversely on the character of a witness on your side of the case.

No rule defines "character evidence." In civil cases, Rule 404 makes character evidence inadmissible in a case-in-chief, unless character is an essential element of the claim (such as in a libel or slander case).

In criminal cases, Rule 404 allows character evidence. The defendant may put on character evidence of his good character, and the prosecutor may use character evidence to rebut, once the character issue is raised. In sexual assault and child molestation cases, the prosecutor may use character evidence even though the defendant does not put his character at issue.

Rule 607 allows the credibility of any witness to be impeached or attacked.

Rule 608 allows you to use character evidence to impeach or attack the credibility of a witness as well as rebut such an impeachment or attack, subject to two limitations. First, the evidence can go only to character for truthfulness or untruthfulness; second, you can't prove specific acts of bad conduct of untruthfulness or good conduct of truthfulness with extrinsic evidence, such as a document.

Rule 609 limits the use of criminal convictions to those punishable by more than a year's imprisonment and those that occurred within the last ten years, unless the crime involved dishonesty or false statement, in which case any conviction that occurred within the last ten years is admissible.

These rules pertain mostly to documents extolling the character of one of your opponent's witnesses when your opponent wants to use that document on direct examination in the case-in-chief. However, if you attack that witness's credibility on cross-examination, your opponent can come back with character evidence on redirect.

The rules also pertain to documents attacking the character of one of your witnesses when your opponent wants to use that document in cross-examination of that witness or in direct examination of another witness who supports the attack on your witness.

Objections to Completeness
Completeness: The Signals

Look for the following types of exhibits:

- text documents;
- recordings.

Look for the following signals on the completeness of an exhibit that is a document or recording.

- Your opponent offers an exhibit that is a multipage document and some of the pages are missing.

- Your opponent offers a document with attachments and one or more of the attachments are missing (or the attachments are multipage documents and some of the pages are missing).

- Your opponent offers a clip from a video or sound recording that is only a part of the entire recording.

Completeness: The Framework

In the federal system, Rule 106 provides:

> If a party introduces all or part of a writing or recorded statement, an adverse party may require the introduction, at that time, of any other part—or any other writing or

recorded statement—that in fairness ought
to be considered at the same time.

The Advisory Committee's notes point out:

> The rule is based on two considerations.
> The first is the misleading impression cre-
> ated by taking matters out of context. The
> second is the inadequacy of repair work
> when delayed to a point later in the trial.
> The rule does not in any way circumscribe
> the right of the adversary to develop the
> matter on cross-examination or as part of
> his own case. For practical reasons, the rule
> is limited to writings and recorded state-
> ments and does not apply to conversations.

Federal Rule of Civil Procedure 32(a)(6) provides a
counterpart specifically for deposition transcripts:

> If a party offers in evidence only part of a
> deposition, an adverse party may require
> the offeror to introduce other parts that in
> fairness should be considered with the part
> introduced, and any party may itself intro-
> duce any other parts.

Most states have similar rules.

Objections to Confusing, Misleading
Confusing, Misleading: The Signals

Look for the following types of exhibits:

- charts, graphs, tables;

- drawings, diagrams, sketches;

- models;

- photographs;

- text documents;

- video and audio recordings.

Look for the following signals in exhibits that may qualify as confusing or misleading.

- Chart has vertical and horizontal axes not labeled with proper form.

- Bar chart shows trend over time (line graphs better for this purpose).

- Pie chart is used to show relatively small differences in size.

- Line graph has horizontal axis not divided into equal increments.

- Timeline emphasizes some events unfairly or uses arguments in labels.

- Table has too much information, not all of which is relevant; misleading labels may also be objectionable.

- Drawing is not accurate in some important detail.

- Diagram has labels that are inaccurate, argumentative, or suggestive.

- Sketch is grossly out of proportion.

- Photograph or video includes a lot of irrelevant matter or excludes a lot of relevant matter at a scene; enlargement confuses the actual size of some object at issue; time lapse may have occurred between the event at issue and the taking of the photo; digital manipulation of the image may change its status as a fair and accurate representation of something.

- Audio recording has portions that are inaudible; transcript is inaccurate.

- Animation with inaccurate or argumentative labels; colors or action different from the "real thing."

- Model that has some parts made to one scale and other parts made to another scale; colors different from the "real thing."

Confusing, Misleading: The Framework

Rule 403 provides: "The court may exclude relevant evidence if its probative value is substantially outweighed by a danger of . . . confusing the issues [or] misleading the jury . . . ."

Objections to Needless Cumulative Evidence, Undue Delay, Wasting Time

Needless Cumulative Evidence: The Signals

Look for the following types of exhibits:

- animations;

- charts, graphs, tables;

- text documents;

- timelines;

- videos.

Look for the following signals in exhibits that may qualify as needlessly cumulative evidence or causing undue delay or wasting time:

- documents that pile on more and more instances of the same conduct;

- charts, graphs, and tables that present repetitive evidence with no new information;

- timelines presented after detailed witness testimony about the times and events depicted on the timeline;

- exhibits that will require substantial time to set up in the courtroom, such as large or bulky items, or that might cause disruption in the courtroom;

- exhibits that will require substantial time to voir dire a witness about the adequacy of the foundation for the exhibit when other evidence on the point involved has already been presented;

- exhibits that will require substantial time to cross-examine the witness about the truthfulness and reliability of the content of the exhibit when other evidence on the point involved has already been presented;

- videos that incorporate photos already in evidence;

- animations that repeat expert testimony.

Needless Cumulative Evidence: The Framework

Rule 403 provides that relevant evidence may be excluded if its probative value is substantially outweighed by a danger of undue delay, wasting time, or needlessly presenting cumulative evidence.

Objections to cumulative evidence with respect to exhibits usually are directed at a large number of separate exhibits used to prove the same fact without adding anything new. In a jury trial, repeating the same fact over and over again can give an unfair emphasis on that fact, while diminishing other equally important facts.

Objections to undue delay and wasting time generally refer to the same kinds of circumstances. An "undue" delay is one that is inappropriate, excessive, unjustified, or unfair. It is a delay that goes beyond the reasonable amount of time customary in a trial of this sort.

Objections to Failure to Meet Original Document Requirements

Original Document Requirements: The Signals

Look for the following types of exhibits:

- writings;
- recordings;
- photographs.

Look for the following signals that may subject such an exhibit to an objection for failure to meet the original document requirements:

- marks or handwriting on a copy of a document that were not on the original;

- a document that is a bad copy—parts faded, blurred, or illegible;

- a handwritten copy of a document that originally was printed or typed;

- a copy of a document that has parts missing that were included in the original;

- a photograph that has been digitally altered;

- a photograph that has marks, labels, handwriting, or other marks on it that were not on the original;

- a copy of a document about which there is a genuine question about the authenticity of the original (e.g., a document with a signature of questioned authenticity that your expert needs the original to make a proper determination);

- a copy of a document under circumstances when it would be unfair to admit the copy (e.g., account books in which it is not possible to determine deletions or omissions in the copy without the original);

- a video recording that is blurred or unclear in parts;

- an audio recording that is inaudible in parts.

Original Document Requirements: The Framework

Rule 1002 provides: "An original writing, recording, or photograph is required in order to prove its content unless these rules or a federal statute provide otherwise."

The rule is usually referred to as the "original document rule" or the "original document requirement." In practice, however, an original is almost never required because nearly all duplicates are acceptable.

Rule 1003 provides that a duplicate is admissible to the same extent as the original unless a genuine question is raised about the original's authenticity or the circumstances make it unfair to admit the duplicate.

Technically, your opponent is required to lay a foundation that demonstrates that the exhibit your opponent seeks to be admitted is a duplicate. Rule 1001(e) defines a duplicate as "a counterpart produced by a mechanical, photographic, chemical, electronic, or other equivalent process or technique that accurately reproduces the original." That requires witness testimony about the process by which the duplicate was made (usually a standard photocopier) and that the process accurately reproduces the original. In practice, experienced lawyers rarely challenge the status or use of an exact duplicate document or photograph. However, they will sometimes challenge duplicates of video and audio recordings just to have a good record in case of later-developed evidence.

Objections are most often directed at copies of documents that are *not* exact duplicates. These documents are copies that have marks or handwriting on them, have labels pasted on them, or are otherwise changed so they are not exact duplicates of the original. Testimony from a witness with firsthand knowledge of the marks, labels, or handwriting is required to qualify a nonduplicate copy of a document.

Rule 1004 allows secondary evidence if the original is lost or unavailable. (In connection with oral testimony about the content of a document, this is sometimes called the "best evidence" rule.) In the case of a nonduplicate copy, even without witness testimony to qualify the marks on a nonduplicate copy, it can be admitted under Rule 1004 if the original is lost or unavailable.

You should *not* object under the original document rules to the following.

- *A summary of voluminous materials.* Under Rule 1006, a summary is itself an exception to the original document rule.

- *A computer printout.* Rule 1001(d) provides: "For electronically stored information, 'original' means any printout—or other output readable by sight—if it accurately reflects the information."

- *An enlargement of an exhibit.* An example would be a blowup of a document on posterboard used with an easel in a courtroom or an enlargement on a digital display. The enlargement is a duplicate even though it is a different size and is admissible to the same extent as the original unless, under Rule 1003, there is something unfair about it.

- *A timeline created for litigation purposes.* It does not matter that there may have been prior versions or whether those prior versions are discoverable. The version used as the exhibit is either an original or a duplicate.

- *Published materials.* Rule 1001(d) provides that "any counterpart intended to have the same effect by the person who executed or issued it" is an original.

- *Drawings diagrams, physical objects or substances, and models.* Under Rule 1001(a) and (b), these are not writings or recordings and are not covered by the requirement of an original.

- *Medical images like CAT scans, MRI images, and x-rays.* These are digital files and Rule 1001(d) provides: "For electronically stored information, 'original' means any printout—or other output readable by sight—if it accurately reflects the information."

- *Material on a digital storage device.* Under Rule 1001(e), material on a digital storage device is a "duplicate" as it is a "counterpart produced by . . . electronic or other process or technique that accurately reproduces the original."

Objections to Parol Evidence
Parol Evidence: The Signals

Look for the following types of exhibits:

- text documents;

- recordings.

Look for the following signals for an objection based on the parol evidence rule:

- content that is evidence of discussions or negotiations prior to the completion of a contract;

- content that is evidence of discussions or negotiations contemporaneous with the completion of the contract;

- content showing, prior to the completion of the contract, what one party or the other wanted or hoped to accomplish with the contract;

- content showing, prior to the completion of the contract, what one party or the other understood with respect to words or terms used in the contract.

Parol Evidence: The Framework

No federal rule sets out the parol evidence rule. This is a common-law rule followed in the federal courts and most state courts that applies only to contracts.

The rule provides, in general, that no forms of extrinsic evidence, including documents, are admissible to prove the terms and conditions of a written contract. Only the contract itself can be used for that purpose.

Objections to Summaries of Voluminous Material

Summary of Voluminous Materials: The Signals

Look for the following types of exhibits that may qualify as a summary of voluminous materials:

- a text document summarizing many pages of documents;

- a chart or table combining data from many sources;

- an animation based on measurements, photographs, operating data, and other kinds of information.

A summary, like any other exhibit, must have a foundation that includes the standard four elements:

1) *Competence of the witness.* The witness must have firsthand knowledge of the underlying materials and the preparation of the summary.

2) *Identification of the exhibit.* The witness must identify the summary sufficiently to differentiate it from any other evidence in the case.

3) *Relevance.* The summary must be relevant to a fact at issue in the case.

4) *Authenticity*. The witness must offer sufficient evidence of the accuracy of the summary in relation to the underlying materials.

An objection to the summary is available if any of the foundation elements are missing.

Summary of Voluminous Materials: The Framework

Rule 1006 provides:

> The proponent may use a summary, chart, or calculation to prove the content of voluminous writings, recordings, or photographs that cannot be conveniently examined in court. The proponent must make the originals or duplicates available for examination or copying, or both, by other parties at a reasonable time and place. And the court may order the proponent to produce them in court.

In addition, the rule requires your opponent to deliver all the underlying materials to you. If you can identify any materials used in the summary that were not made available, then you have a good objection to any use of that summary. If the underlying materials were not delivered at a time sufficiently in advance of the deposition or trial to allow you to effectively prepare a cross-examination, then there is also a good objection to any use of the summary.

Objection to Surprise at Trial
Surprise: The Signals

Look for the following signals for an objection based on surprise.

- Any exhibit that was required to be produced in discovery, but was not produced, and turns up for the first time at trial.

- Any exhibit that is subject to a pretrial order and does not comply with the order. Such exhibits include:

  - displays to be used in opening statement or closing argument;

  - exhibits to be premarked;

  - exhibits to be listed on a pretrial exhibit list and exchanged.

Surprise: The Framework

No rule covers this objection in specific terms. Rule 611(a) covers the general proposition that a party should have a fair chance to deal with an exhibit and should not be ambushed at trial.

You can object to any exhibit that was not disclosed in discovery or other pretrial proceedings on the grounds of "surprise." Whether you are actually "surprised" or not, there are important policy objectives at stake in securing fair and adequate disclosure in pre-trial proceedings. This objection might also be made under Rule 403—unfair prejudice.

Objections to Unfair Prejudice
Unfair Prejudice: The Signals

Look for the following kinds of exhibits.

- Documents that will create an adverse impression of the witness, but are not centrally relevant to the issues in the case:

    - moral character, such as excessive drinking, gambling, drug use, sexual activity;

    - physical violence, such as fighting, beatings, child abuse.

- Documents, photographs, and videos that contain shocking content:

    - sexually explicit material;

    - indecent, lewd, or obscene material.

- Photographs, videos, and drawings that are gruesome:

    - facial expressions of great pain;

    - oozing wounds;

    - shattered skulls;

    - severed body parts;

    - dead bodies.

Unfair Prejudice: The Framework

Rule 403 provides that relevant evidence may be excluded if its probative value is substantially outweighed by a danger of unfair prejudice.

The commentary to the rule points out that "unfair prejudice" means an undue tendency to suggest decision on an improper basis—commonly, though not necessarily, an emotional one.

This is an objection you would use primarily in jury trials. Inflammatory testimony may arouse emotions—such as sympathy, disgust, anger, or revulsion—to such an extent that the rational process of the jurors' considerations of the evidence may be disrupted. Judges expect that objections to matters of unfair prejudice will be dealt with by pretrial motions in limine.

PART THREE: RECOGNIZING OTHER SPECIALIZED OBJECTIONS AT TRIAL

This section covers objections you can use at trial to deal with aspects of the process other than oral testimony and exhibits. They are the available objections to:

- opening statements;
- judicial notice;
- presumptions;
- closing arguments.

With respect to each of these categories of potential objections, this part supplies a brief background orientation along with descriptions of the particular objections that may apply. Most experienced trial lawyers use these objections only rarely. They are outliers that arise occasionally in specialized circumstances.

There are other even more specialized objections sometimes available:

- voir dire in selecting a jury;
- jury site visits and the terms and conditions under which a site visit is conducted;
- jury instructions.

The choice to lodge these objections depends highly on the facts and circumstances of a particular case and therefore are not discussed here.

There are also objections to the conduct of the judge. The American Bar Association's Model Code of Judicial Conduct Rule 2.3(B) collects most of the bases on which objections to the conduct of judges have been sustained in the past. Canon 3A of the Code of Conduct for United States Judges, adopted by the Judicial Conference of the United States, also sets out general rules of judicial conduct. For obvious reasons, objections to the conduct of a judge during a trial are very rare, and this subject is not covered here.

Opening Statements
Background

The purpose of the opening statement is for the lawyers to preview the facts they intend to prove in their case either through oral testimony or exhibits. Most of the objections to opening statements are derived from common-law practice. However, the ethics rules also affect opening statements. Rule 3.4 of the ABA Model Rules of Professional Conduct provides:

> A lawyer shall not . . . (e) in trial, allude to any matter that the lawyer does not reasonably believe is relevant or that will not be supported by admissible evidence, assert personal knowledge of facts in issue except when testifying as a witness, or state a personal opinion as to the justness of a cause, the credibility of a witness, the culpability of a civil litigant or the guilt or innocence of an accused.

Available Objections to Opening Statements

Look for the following cues that you have an available objection.

1) Addressing an individual juror. Jurors may be addressed by name only during voir dire of the jury.

2) Anticipating a defense. Some judges limit an opening statement to what counsel intends to prove, and these judges may rule that counsel cannot openly deal with the weakness of an opponent's contentions because this is "argument."

3) Argument.

   • Stating facts as established rather than with a preface such as "the evidence will show" or "we will prove that"—formulations that are acceptable.

   • Interpreting or characterizing the facts—presenting the facts to be proven during the trial is permissible, presenting counsel's theory of the facts is not.

   • Addressing the credibility of witnesses or the comparative weight of the evidence.

4) Stating "facts" that can't be proved. The ethics rule requires that counsel have a good-faith belief that what they state has a basis in law or fact.

5) Violating pretrial motions in limine. If the court has ruled in pretrial proceedings that evidence is not admissible or that other restrictions apply to opening statements,

those rulings will enforced during opening statements.

6) Mentioning excludable material. Rules 407–411 exclude subsequent remedial measures, liability insurance, offers of compromise, offers to pay medical expenses, and pleas and plea discussions. None of these may be mentioned in an opening.

7) Instructing on the principles of law.

- Discussing the law governing the case generally is objectionable, but the court usually will allow counsel to refer to legal principles if the reference is brief and accurate.

- Once the lawyer has discussed the facts with respect to the conduct of a party in the case, she may talk about how this conduct violated law or regulations in specific ways. Usually a statement that "the defendant failed to act in accordance with the law" is acceptable. The basic problem here is that references to the law are usually argument, which is not allowed in opening statements.

8) Misstating the law or quoting the law incorrectly.

9) Arguing what the law should be.

10) Referring to irrelevant matters.

11) Discussing side disputes that are not directly relevant to the central dispute in the case.

12) Giving counsel's personal beliefs, including the credibility or veracity of witnesses, the justness of the cause, or the validity of the case.

13) Presenting counsel's personal knowledge or personal credentials.

14) Engaging in personal attacks on opposing counsel or witnesses.

15) Referring to unfairly prejudicial matters:

- financial circumstances, wealth, or poverty of a party or witness;

- appeals to race, nationality, or religion;

- prior acts of misconduct of a party.

The decision whether to make an objection during opening statement depends on your planned strategy and tactics for the case. However, the most-often cited rule of thumb of experienced trial lawyers is that if you are going to object during opening statement, you have to win. That is why it is important to

---

remember that judges have personal preferences about how they will rule on objections to openings. Be sure to research what your judge has done in the past.

Judicial Notice
Background

Judicial notice is the court's acceptance of an adjudicative fact so that your opponent does not need to offer proof of the fact.

In the federal system, Rule 201 deals with judicial notice of adjudicative facts. An adjudicative fact is one of the facts at issue in the particular case.

This is distinguished from a "legislative fact," which the Advisory Committee's note to Rule 201 describes as "those which have relevance to legal reasoning and the lawmaking process, whether in the formulation of a legal principle or ruling by a judge or court or in the enactment of a legislative body." These are the kinds of facts from cited authority that the parties put in their briefs and judges put in their opinions. There is no rule governing legislative facts.

Rule 201(b) provides:

> The court may judicially notice a fact that is not subject to reasonable dispute because it:
>
> (1) is generally known within the trial court's territorial jurisdiction; or
>
> (2) can be accurately and readily determined from sources whose accuracy cannot be reasonably questioned.

Judicial notice does not have anything to do with whether the judge has any personal knowledge of the fact that is noticed. The idea is that when a fact is generally known and not disputed, it would be a waste of time to require one of the parties to prove that fact.

Judicial notice is discretionary with the court. The court may act on its own motion or at the request of a party. A judge may always require the party to prove the fact, and it is never error for the court to decline to take judicial notice.

The court may act in this regard at any stage of the proceeding. Normally, one party or the other requests the court to take judicial notice, and the court gives the parties an opportunity to be heard. Rule 201 provides that if the court takes action on its own motion and there is no prior notification, a party may request an opportunity to be heard after judicial notice has been taken.

Judicial notice can have an important impact because the court will instruct the jurors to accept as conclusive any fact judicially noticed.

Courts typically take judicial notice of court records of the court where the judge sits, geographic facts in standard reference works, and facts from almanacs, calendars, periodic tables, and the like. The Advisory Committee Notes point out that "[t]he usual method of establishing adjudicative facts is through the introduction of evidence, ordinarily consisting of the testimony of witnesses. If particular facts are outside of reasonable controversy, this process is dispensed with as unnecessary. A high degree of indisputability is the essential prerequisite."

In the federal system, judges do not take judicial notice of foreign law; rather, they make a specific ruling. Federal Rule of Civil Procedure 44.1 provides that a party intending to raise an issue about a foreign country's law must give notice to the other side. Then the court can consider any relevant material or source, including testimony. These sources need not be submitted by a party or admissible under the Federal Rules of Evidence.

Available Objections to Judicial Notice

You will generally object to one of the following.

1) The fact to be judicially noticed is not generally known in the jurisdiction.

2) The fact to be judicially noticed is disputed.

3) Authoritative sources differ as to the fact, so they cannot readily be verified from an authoritative source.

Presumptions
Background

A presumption establishes a fact in a matter until sufficient evidence is introduced to prove the contrary. In essence, a presumption is a fact assumed to be true under the law. The presumption can be made and relied on without any proof. Presumptions have their basis in common law, but some are now established by state and federal statutes. In the federal system, Rule 301 provides:

> [T]he party against whom a presumption is directed has the burden of producing evidence to rebut the presumption.

The Advisory Committee Notes explain that "presumptions governed by this rule are given the effect of placing upon the opposing party the burden of establishing the nonexistence of the presumed fact, once the party invoking the presumption establishes the basic facts giving rise to it."

Presumptions are used to relieve a party from having to prove the truth of the fact being presumed. Once a party relies on a presumption, however, the other party may offer evidence to rebut or disprove the presumption. In effect, what a presumption really does is place the obligation of presenting evidence concerning a particular fact on a particular party.

Rule 302 provides: "In a civil case, state law governs the effect of a presumption regarding a claim or defense for which state law supplies the rule of decision."

Common-law presumptions include the following.

- *Presumption of innocence.* An accused is presumed innocent until proven guilty.

- *Presumption of death.* A person who has been absent for seven years without explanation is presumed dead. The time period it takes for this presumption to arise often has been modified by statute.

- *Presumption of mail delivery.* A properly addressed letter delivered to the post office or a common carrier is presumed to have been delivered and received by the addressee.

- *Presumption of validity.* The official acts of courts are presumed to be valid.

State law may make other presumptions available.

Available Objections to Presumptions

You will generally rely on one of the following objections.

1) The claim (or defense) to which opposing counsel seeks to apply a presumption is one

under which state law supplies the rule of decision, and the law of this state does not recognize this presumption.

2) The presumption should not be allowed because no notice was given, either in pleadings or at trial, that counsel would rely on a presumption. Federal Rules 301 and 302 do not specifically require notice, but parties usually base this objection on Rule 102 ("These rules should be construed so as to administer every proceeding fairly . . . ") to the effect that without notice, there is no fair opportunity to examine the presumption and formulate an objection.

Closing Argument
Background

You and your opponent have broad areas that you can cover in a closing argument:

- any issue in the case;

- any evidence in the case;

- any reasonable inference from the evidence;

- any argument that is fair;

- any matters of common knowledge.

Available Objections to Closing Argument

Listen for the following objectionable material:

1) Misstating or misquoting the law.

2) Arguing to the jury what the law *should* be.

3) Stating facts that are outside the record.

4) Misstating evidence.

5) Mentioning excluded evidence—evidence excluded by ruling of the court (e.g., unfair prejudice, hearsay) or subject matter excluded by the rules (e.g., subsequent remedial measures, liability insurance).

6) Addressing a juror by name.

7) Making a "golden rule" argument—asking jurors to put themselves in the place of a party or to treat a party as the jurors would like to be treated themselves.

8) Engaging in a personal attack on counsel, a party, a witness.

9) Stating counsel's personal belief of counsel—"I think" or "I believe" arguments.

10) Stating counsel's personal knowledge.

Most of these objections are also available at opening statement and are explained in more detail in the section above.

Trial lawyers often advise not to make objections during an opponent's closing argument. By the time you reach closing argument, you object only if opposing counsel violates the law or fair practice with respect to closing argument and the violation seriously hurts your client. And it is maximally important to object only when you are confident that the judge will sustain the objection. The end of the case is not the place to be overruled.

SUMMARY LIST OF OBJECTIONS

Oral Testimony
Potential Objections to Questions

Ambiguous

Argumentative

Asked and answered

Assumes facts not in evidence

Badgering the witness

Best evidence rule, violation

Beyond the scope of direct or cross

Character evidence, improper

Characterizing of evidence, improper

Compound

Conclusion

Confusing

Cumulative evidence, needless

Embarrassing the witness, unreasonably

Foundation, lack of

Habit and routine evidence, improper

Harassing the witness

Hearsay

Impeachment, improper

Irrelevant or immaterial

Leading

Liability insurance

Misleads the witness

Misquotes the witness

Misstates the evidence

Narrative, calls for

Offer of compromise

Offer to pay medical expenses

Opinion by lay witness, improper

Opinion by expert witness, improper

Oppressing the witness, unreasonably

Parol evidence rule, violation

Plea or plea discussion

Privileged communication

Refreshing recollection, improper

Speculation

Subsequent remedial measures

Telephone call, not authenticated

Undue delay

Unfair prejudice

Unintelligible

Vague

Wasting time

Witness lacks personal knowledge

Potential Objections to Answers

Best evidence rule, violation

Character evidence, improper

Characterizing of evidence, improper

Conclusion

Foundation, lack of

Hearsay

Irrelevant or immaterial

Liability insurance

Misstates evidence

Narrative

Nonresponsive to question asked

Offer of compromise

Offer to pay medical expenses

Opinion by a lay witness, improper

Parol evidence rule, violation

Plea or plea discussion

Privileged information

Speculation

Subsequent remedial measure

Telephone call, not authenticated

Unfair prejudice (inflammatory)

Volunteered information

Exhibits
Potential Objections to Foundation

Competence (personal knowledge) of the witness

Identification of the exhibit

Relevance of the exhibit

Authentication of the exhibit

Potential Objections to Content

Character evidence, improper

Completeness

Conclusion

Confusing

Cumulative evidence, needless

Hearsay

Liability insurance

Misleading

Offer of compromise

Offer to pay medical expenses

Opinion, lay witness

Original document requirements

Parol evidence

Plea or plea discussion

Prior statement of a witness, improper use

Privileged communication

Subsequent remedial measures

Speculation

Summary of voluminous material, requirements

Surprise

Undue delay

Unfair prejudice

Wasting time

Appendix A

FEDERAL RULES OF EVIDENCE

for United States Courts and
Magistrates

Approved January 2, 1975
Effective July 1, 1975
As amended to December 1, 2017

Contents

Federal Rules of Evidence

ARTICLE I—GENERAL PROVISIONS

Rule 101. Scope; Definitions

(a) **Scope.** These rules apply to proceedings in United States courts. The specific courts and proceedings to which the rules apply, along with exceptions, are set out in Rule 1101.

(b) **Definitions.** In these rules:

    (1) "civil case" means a civil action or proceeding;

    (2) "criminal case" includes a criminal proceeding;

    (3) "public office" includes a public agency;

    (4) "record" includes a memorandum, report, or data compilation;

    (5) a "rule prescribed by the Supreme Court" means a rule adopted by the Supreme Court under statutory authority; and

    (6) a reference to any kind of written material or any other medium includes electronically stored information.

Rule 102.   Purpose

These rules should be construed so as to administer every proceeding fairly, eliminate unjustifiable expense and delay, and promote the development of evidence law, to the end of ascertaining the truth and securing a just determination.

Rule 103.   Rulings on Evidence

(a)   **Preserving a Claim of Error.** A party may claim error in a ruling to admit or exclude evidence only if the error affects a substantial right of the party and:

    (1)   if the ruling admits evidence, a party, on the record:

        (A)   timely objects or moves to strike; and

        (B)   states the specific ground, unless it was apparent from the context; or

    (2)   if the ruling excludes evidence, a party informs the court of its substance by an offer of proof, unless the substance was apparent from the context.

(b)   **Not Needing to Renew an Objection or Offer of Proof.** Once the court rules definitively on the record—either before or at trial—a party need not renew an objection or offer of proof to preserve a claim of error for appeal.

(c)   **Court's Statement About the Ruling; Directing an Offer of Proof.** The court may make any statement about the character or form of the evidence, the objection made, and the ruling. The court may direct that an offer of proof be made in question-and-answer form.

(d)   **Preventing the Jury from Hearing Inadmissible Evidence.** To the extent practicable, the court must conduct a jury trial so that inadmissible evidence is not suggested to the jury by any means.

(e)   **Taking Notice of Plain Error.** A court may take notice of a plain error affecting a substantial right, even if the claim of error was not properly preserved.

Rule 104.   Preliminary Questions

(a)   **In General.** The court must decide any preliminary question about whether a witness is qualified, a privilege exists, or evidence is admissible. In so deciding, the court is not bound by evidence rules, except those on privilege.

(b)   **Relevance That Depends on a Fact.** When the relevance of evidence depends on whether a fact exists, proof must be introduced sufficient to support a finding that the fact does exist. The court may admit the proposed evidence on the condition that the proof be introduced later.

(c)   **Conducting a Hearing So That the Jury Cannot Hear It.** The court must conduct any hearing on a preliminary question so that the jury cannot hear it if:

(1)   the hearing involves the admissibility of a confession;

(2)   a defendant in a criminal case is a witness and so requests; or

(3)   justice so requires.

(d)   **Cross-Examining a Defendant in a Criminal Case.** By testifying on a preliminary question, a defendant in a criminal case does not become subject to cross-examination on other issues in the case.

(e)   **Evidence Relevant to Weight and Credibility.** This rule does not limit a party's right to introduce before the jury evidence that is relevant to the weight or credibility of other evidence.

Rule 105.   Limiting Evidence That Is Not Admissible Against Other Parties or for Other Purposes

If the court admits evidence that is admissible against a party or for a purpose—but not against another party or for another purpose—the court, on timely request, must restrict the evidence to its proper scope and instruct the jury accordingly.

Rule 106.   Remainder of or Related Writings or Recorded Statements

If a party introduces all or part of a writing or recorded statement, an adverse party may require the introduction, at that time, of any other part—or any other writing or recorded statement—that in fairness ought to be considered at the same time.

ARTICLE II—JUDICIAL NOTICE

Rule 201.   Judicial Notice of Adjudicative Facts

(a)   **Scope.** This rule governs judicial notice of an adjudicative fact only, not a legislative fact.

(b)   **Kinds of Facts That May Be Judicially Noticed.** The court may judicially notice a fact that is not subject to reasonable dispute because it:

    (1)   is generally known within the trial court's territorial jurisdiction; or

    (2)   can be accurately and readily determined from sources whose accuracy cannot reasonably be questioned.

(c)   **Taking Notice.** The court:

    (1)   may take judicial notice on its own; or

    (2)   must take judicial notice if a party requests it and the court is supplied with the necessary information.

(d)   **Timing.** The court may take judicial notice at any stage of the proceeding.

(e)   **Opportunity to Be Heard.** On timely request, a party is entitled to be heard on the propriety of taking judicial notice and the nature of the fact to be noticed. If the court takes judicial notice before notifying a party, the party, on request, is still entitled to be heard.

(f)   **Instructing the Jury.** In a civil case, the court must instruct the jury to accept the noticed fact as conclusive. In a criminal case, the court must instruct the jury that it may or may not accept the noticed fact as conclusive.

ARTICLE III—PRESUMPTIONS IN CIVIL CASES

Rule 301.   Presumptions in Civil Cases Generally

In a civil case, unless a federal statute or these rules provide otherwise, the party against whom a presumption is directed has the burden of producing evidence to rebut the presumption. But this rule does not shift the burden of persuasion, which remains on the party who had it originally.

Rule 302.   Applying State Law to Presumptions in Civil Cases

In a civil case, state law governs the effect of a presumption regarding a claim or defense for which state law supplies the rule of decision.

ARTICLE IV—RELEVANCE AND ITS LIMITS

Rule 401.   Test for Relevant Evidence

Evidence is relevant if:

(a)   it has any tendency to make a fact more or less probable than it would be without the evidence; and

(b)   the fact is of consequence in determining the action.

Rule 402.   General Admissibility of Relevant Evidence

Relevant evidence is admissible unless any of the following provides otherwise:

- the United States Constitution;
- a federal statute;
- these rules; or
- other rules prescribed by the Supreme Court.

Irrelevant evidence is not admissible.

Rule 403.   Excluding Relevant Evidence for Prejudice, Confusion, Waste of Time, or Other Reasons

The court may exclude relevant evidence if its probative value is substantially outweighed by a danger of one or more of the following: unfair prejudice, confusing the issues, misleading the jury, undue delay, wasting time, or needlessly presenting cumulative evidence.

Rule 404.   Character Evidence; Crimes or Other Acts

(a)   Character Evidence.

(1)   *Prohibited Uses.* Evidence of a person's character or character trait is not admissible to prove that on a particular occasion the person acted in accordance with the character or trait.

(2) *Exceptions for a Defendant or Victim in a Criminal Case.* The following exceptions apply in a criminal case:

    (A) a defendant may offer evidence of the defendant's pertinent trait, and if the evidence is admitted, the prosecutor may offer evidence to rebut it;

    (B) subject to the limitations in Rule 412, a defendant may offer evidence of an alleged victim's pertinent trait, and if the evidence is admitted, the prosecutor may:

        (i) offer evidence to rebut it; and

        (ii) offer evidence of the defendant's same trait; and

    (C) in a homicide case, the prosecutor may offer evidence of the alleged victim's trait of peacefulness to rebut evidence that the victim was the first aggressor.

(3) *Exceptions for a Witness.* Evidence of a witness's character may be admitted under Rules 607, 608, and 609.

(b) **Crimes, Wrongs, or Other Acts.**

(1) *Prohibited Uses.* Evidence of a crime, wrong, or other act is not admissible to prove a person's character in order to show that on a particular occasion the person acted in accordance with the character.

(2) *Permitted Uses; Notice in a Criminal Case.* This evidence may be admissible for another purpose, such as proving motive, opportunity, intent, preparation, plan, knowledge, identity, absence of mistake, or lack of accident. On request by a defendant in a criminal case, the prosecutor must:

(A) provide reasonable notice of the general nature of any such evidence that the prosecutor intends to offer at trial; and

(B) do so before trial—or during trial if the court, for good cause, excuses lack of pretrial notice.

Rule 405.   Methods of Proving Character

(a) **By Reputation or Opinion.** When evidence of a person's character or character trait is admissible, it may be proved by testimony about the person's reputation or by testimony in the form of an opinion. On cross-examination of the character witness, the court may allow an inquiry into relevant specific instances of the person's conduct.

(b) **By Specific Instances of Conduct.** When a person's character or character trait is an essential element of a charge, claim, or defense, the character or trait may also be proved by relevant specific instances of the person's conduct.

Rule 406. Habit; Routine Practice

Evidence of a person's habit or an organization's routine practice may be admitted to prove that on a particular occasion the person or organization acted in accordance with the habit or routine practice. The court may admit this evidence regardless of whether it is corroborated or whether there was an eyewitness.

Rule 407. Subsequent Remedial Measures

When measures are taken that would have made an earlier injury or harm less likely to occur, evidence of the subsequent measures is not admissible to prove:

- negligence;
- culpable conduct;
- a defect in a product or its design; or
- a need for a warning or instruction.

But the court may admit this evidence for another purpose, such as impeachment or—if disputed—proving ownership, control, or the feasibility of precautionary measures.

Rule 408. Compromise Offers and Negotiations

(a) **Prohibited Uses.** Evidence of the following is not admissible—on behalf of any party—either to prove or disprove the validity or amount of a disputed claim or to impeach by a prior inconsistent statement or a contradiction:

(1)   furnishing, promising, or offering—or accepting, promising to accept, or offering to accept—a valuable consideration in compromising or attempting to compromise the claim; and

(2)   conduct or a statement made during compromise negotiations about the claim—except when offered in a criminal case and when the negotiations related to a claim by a public office in the exercise of its regulatory, investigative, or enforcement authority.

(b)   **Exceptions.** The court may admit this evidence for another purpose, such as proving a witness's bias or prejudice, negating a contention of undue delay, or proving an effort to obstruct a criminal investigation or prosecution.

Rule 409.   Offers to Pay Medical and Similar Expenses

Evidence of furnishing, promising to pay, or offering to pay medical, hospital, or similar expenses resulting from an injury is not admissible to prove liability for the injury.

Rule 410.   Pleas, Plea Discussions, and Related Statements

(a)   **Prohibited Uses.** In a civil or criminal case, evidence of the following is not admissible against the defendant who made the plea or participated in the plea discussions:

(1) a guilty plea that was later withdrawn;

(2) a nolo contendere plea;

(3) a statement made during a proceeding on either of those pleas under Federal Rule of Criminal Procedure 11 or a comparable state procedure; or

(4) a statement made during plea discussions with an attorney for the prosecuting authority if the discussions did not result in a guilty plea or they resulted in a later-withdrawn guilty plea.

(b) **Exceptions.** The court may admit a statement described in Rule 410(a)(3) or (4):

(1) in any proceeding in which another statement made during the same plea or plea discussions has been introduced, if in fairness the statements ought to be considered together; or

(2) in a criminal proceeding for perjury or false statement, if the defendant made the statement under oath, on the record, and with counsel present.

Rule 411.   Liability Insurance

Evidence that a person was or was not insured against liability is not admissible to prove whether the person acted negligently or otherwise wrongfully. But the court may admit this evidence for another purpose, such as proving a witness's bias or prejudice or proving agency, ownership, or control.

Rule 412. Sex-Offense Cases: The Victim's Sexual Behavior or Predisposition

(a) **Prohibited Uses.** The following evidence is not admissible in a civil or criminal proceeding involving alleged sexual misconduct:

    (1) evidence offered to prove that a victim engaged in other sexual behavior; or

    (2) evidence offered to prove a victim's sexual predisposition.

(b) **Exceptions.**

    (1) *Criminal Cases.* The court may admit the following evidence in a criminal case:

        (A) evidence of specific instances of a victim's sexual behavior, if offered to prove that someone other than the defendant was the source of semen, injury, or other physical evidence;

        (B) evidence of specific instances of a victim's sexual behavior with respect to the person accused of the sexual misconduct, if offered by the defendant to prove consent or if offered by the prosecutor; and

        (C) evidence whose exclusion would violate the defendant's constitutional rights.

(2) *Civil Cases.* In a civil case, the court may admit evidence offered to prove a victim's sexual behavior or sexual predisposition if its probative value substantially outweighs the danger of harm to any victim and of unfair prejudice to any party. The court may admit evidence of a victim's reputation only if the victim has placed it in controversy.

(c) **Procedure to Determine Admissibility.**

(1) *Motion.* If a party intends to offer evidence under Rule 412(b), the party must:

(A) file a motion that specifically describes the evidence and states the purpose for which it is to be offered;

(B) do so at least 14 days before trial unless the court, for good cause, sets a different time;

(C) serve the motion on all parties; and

(D) notify the victim or, when appropriate, the victim's guardian or representative.

(2) *Hearing.* Before admitting evidence under this rule, the court must conduct an in camera hearing and give the victim and parties a right to attend and be heard. Unless the court orders otherwise, the motion, related materials, and the record of the hearing must be and remain sealed.

(d) **Definition of "Victim."** In this rule, "victim" includes an alleged victim.

Rule 413.   Similar Crimes in Sexual-Assault Cases

(a)   **Permitted Uses.** In a criminal case in which a defendant is accused of a sexual assault, the court may admit evidence that the defendant committed any other sexual assault. The evidence may be considered on any matter to which it is relevant.

(b)   **Disclosure to the Defendant.** If the prosecutor intends to offer this evidence, the prosecutor must disclose it to the defendant, including witnesses' statements or a summary of the expected testimony. The prosecutor must do so at least 15 days before trial or at a later time that the court allows for good cause.

(c)   **Effect on Other Rules.** This rule does not limit the admission or consideration of evidence under any other rule.

(d)   **Definition of "Sexual Assault."** In this rule and Rule 415, "sexual assault" means a crime under federal law or under state law (as "state" is defined in 18 U.S.C. § 513) involving:

(1)   any conduct prohibited by 18 U.S.C. chapter 109A;

(2)   contact, without consent, between any part of the defendant's body—or an object—and another person's genitals or anus;

(3)   contact, without consent, between the defendant's genitals or anus and any part of another person's body;

(4)   deriving sexual pleasure or gratification from inflicting death, bodily injury, or physical pain on another person; or

(5)   an attempt or conspiracy to engage in conduct described in subparagraphs (1)–(4).

Rule 414.   Similar Crimes in Child-Molestation Cases

(a)   **Permitted Uses.** In a criminal case in which a defendant is accused of child molestation, the court may admit evidence that the defendant committed any other child molestation. The evidence may be considered on any matter to which it is relevant.

(b)   **Disclosure to the Defendant.** If the prosecutor intends to offer this evidence, the prosecutor must disclose it to the defendant, including witnesses' statements or a summary of the expected testimony. The prosecutor must do so at least 15 days before trial or at a later time that the court allows for good cause.

(c)   **Effect on Other Rules.** This rule does not limit the admission or consideration of evidence under any other rule.

(d)   **Definition of "Child" and "Child Molestation."**

In this rule and Rule 415:

(1)   "child" means a person below the age of 14; and

(2) "child molestation" means a crime under federal law or under state law (as "state" is defined in 18 U.S.C. § 513) involving:

    (A) any conduct prohibited by 18 U.S.C. chapter 109A and committed with a child;

    (B) any conduct prohibited by 18 U.S.C. chapter 110;

    (C) contact between any part of the defendant's body—or an object—and a child's genitals or anus;

    (D) contact between the defendant's genitals or anus and any part of a child's body;

    (E) deriving sexual pleasure or gratification from inflicting death, bodily injury, or physical pain on a child; or

    (F) an attempt or conspiracy to engage in conduct described in subparagraphs (A)–(E).

Rule 415. Similar Acts in Civil Cases Involving Sexual Assault or Child Molestation

(a) **Permitted Uses.** In a civil case involving a claim for relief based on a party's alleged sexual assault or child molestation, the court may admit evidence that the party committed any other sexual assault or child molestation. The evidence may be considered as provided in Rules 413 and 414.

(b) **Disclosure to the Opponent.** If a party intends to offer this evidence, the party must disclose it to the party against whom it will be offered, including witnesses' statements or a summary of the expected testimony. The party must do so at least 15 days before trial or at a later time that the court allows for good cause.

(c) **Effect on Other Rules.** This rule does not limit the admission or consideration of evidence under any other rule.

ARTICLE V—PRIVILEGES

Rule 501.   Privilege in General

The common law—as interpreted by United States courts in the light of reason and experience—governs a claim of privilege unless any of the following provides otherwise:

- the United States Constitution;

- a federal statute; or

- rules prescribed by the Supreme Court.

But in a civil case, state law governs privilege regarding a claim or defense for which state law supplies the rule of decision.

Rule 502.   Attorney-Client Privilege and Work Product;
              Limitations on Waiver

The following provisions apply, in the circumstances set out, to disclosure of a communication or information covered by the attorney-client privilege or work-product protection.

(a)   **Disclosure Made in a Federal Proceeding or to a Federal Office or Agency; Scope of a Waiver.** When the disclosure is made in a federal proceeding or to a federal office or agency and waives the attorney-client privilege or work-product protection, the waiver extends to an undisclosed communication or information in a federal or state proceeding only if:

      (1)   the waiver is intentional;

      (2)   the disclosed and undisclosed communications or information concern the same subject matter; and

      (3)   they ought in fairness to be considered together.

(b)   **Inadvertent Disclosure.** When made in a federal proceeding or to a federal office or agency, the disclosure does not operate as a waiver in a federal or state proceeding if:

      (1)   the disclosure is inadvertent;

      (2)   the holder of the privilege or protection took reasonable steps to prevent disclosure; and

---

> > (3) the holder promptly took reasonable steps to rectify the error, including (if applicable) following Federal Rule of Civil Procedure 26(b)(5)(B).

(c) **Disclosure Made in a State Proceeding.** When the disclosure is made in a state proceeding and is not the subject of a state-court order concerning waiver, the disclosure does not operate as a waiver in a federal proceeding if the disclosure:

> (1) would not be a waiver under this rule if it had been made in a federal proceeding; or

> (2) is not a waiver under the law of the state where the disclosure occurred.

(d) **Controlling Effect of a Court Order.** A federal court may order that the privilege or protection is not waived by disclosure connected with the litigation pending before the court—in which event the disclosure is also not a waiver in any other federal or state proceeding.

(e) **Controlling Effect of a Party Agreement.** An agreement on the effect of disclosure in a federal proceeding is binding only on the parties to the agreement, unless it is incorporated into a court order.

(f) **Controlling Effect of this Rule.** Notwithstanding Rules 101 and 1101, this rule applies to state proceedings and to federal court-annexed and federal court-mandated arbitration proceedings, in the circumstances set out in the rule. And notwithstanding

Rule 501, this rule applies even if state law provides the rule of decision.

(g) **Definitions.** In this rule:

   (1)   "attorney-client privilege" means the protection that applicable law provides for confidential attorney-client communications; and

   (2)   "work-product protection" means the protection that applicable law provides for tangible material (or its intangible equivalent) prepared in anticipation of litigation or for trial.

ARTICLE VI —WITNESSES

Rule 601.   Competency to Testify in General

Every person is competent to be a witness unless these rules provide otherwise. But in a civil case, state law governs the witness's competency regarding a claim or defense for which state law supplies the rule of decision.

Rule 602.   Need for Personal Knowledge

A witness may testify to a matter only if evidence is introduced sufficient to support a finding that the witness has personal knowledge of the matter. Evidence to prove personal knowledge may consist of the witness's own testimony. This rule does not apply to a witness's expert testimony under Rule 703.

Rule 603. Oath or Affirmation to Testify Truthfully

Before testifying, a witness must give an oath or affirmation to testify truthfully. It must be in a form designed to impress that duty on the witness's conscience.

Rule 604. Interpreter

An interpreter must be qualified and must give an oath or affirmation to make a true translation.

Rule 605. Judge's Competency as a Witness

The presiding judge may not testify as a witness at the trial. A party need not object to preserve the issue.

Rule 606. Juror's Competency as a Witness

(a) **At the Trial.** A juror may not testify as a witness before the other jurors at the trial. If a juror is called to testify, the court must give a party an opportunity to object outside the jury's presence.

(b) **During an Inquiry into the Validity of a Verdict or Indictment.**

   (1) *Prohibited Testimony or Other Evidence.* During an inquiry into the validity of a verdict or indictment, a juror may not testify about any statement made or incident that occurred during the jury's deliberations; the effect of anything on that juror's or another juror's vote; or any juror's mental processes

concerning the verdict or indictment. The court may not receive a juror's affidavit or evidence of a juror's statement on these matters.

(2) *Exceptions.* A juror may testify about whether:

(A) extraneous prejudicial information was improperly brought to the jury's attention;

(B) an outside influence was improperly brought to bear on any juror; or

(C) a mistake was made in entering the verdict on the verdict form.

Rule 607.   Who May Impeach a Witness

Any party, including the party that called the witness, may attack the witness's credibility.

Rule 608.   A Witness's Character for Truthfulness or Untruthfulness

(a) **Reputation or Opinion Evidence.** A witness's credibility may be attacked or supported by testimony about the witness's reputation for having a character for truthfulness or untruthfulness, or by testimony in the form of an opinion about that character. But evidence of truthful character is admissible only after the witness's character for truthfulness has been attacked.

(b) **Specific Instances of Conduct.** Except for a criminal conviction under Rule 609, extrinsic evidence is not admissible to prove specific instances of a witness's conduct in order to attack or support the witness's character for truthfulness. But the court may, on cross-examination, allow them to be inquired into if they are probative of the character for truthfulness or untruthfulness of:

(1)   the witness; or

(2)   another witness whose character the witness being cross-examined has testified about.

By testifying on another matter, a witness does not waive any privilege against self-incrimination for testimony that relates only to the witness's character for truthfulness.

Rule 609.   Impeachment by Evidence of a Criminal Conviction

(a)   **In General.** The following rules apply to attacking a witness's character for truthfulness by evidence of a criminal conviction:

(1)   for a crime that, in the convicting jurisdiction, was punishable by death or by imprisonment for more than one year, the evidence:

(A)   must be admitted, subject to Rule 403, in a civil case or in a criminal case in which the witness is not a defendant; and

(B)   must be admitted in a criminal case in which the witness is a defendant,

> if the probative value of the evidence outweighs its prejudicial effect to that defendant; and

(2) for any crime regardless of the punishment, the evidence must be admitted if the court can readily determine that establishing the elements of the crime required proving—or the witness's admitting—a dishonest act or false statement.

(b) **Limit on Using the Evidence After 10 Years.** This subdivision (b) applies if more than 10 years have passed since the witness's conviction or release from confinement for it, whichever is later. Evidence of the conviction is admissible only if:

(1) its probative value, supported by specific facts and circumstances, substantially outweighs its prejudicial effect; and

(2) the proponent gives an adverse party reasonable written notice of the intent to use it so that the party has a fair opportunity to contest its use.

(c) **Effect of a Pardon, Annulment, or Certificate of Rehabilitation.** Evidence of a conviction is not admissible if:

(1) the conviction has been the subject of a pardon, annulment, certificate of rehabilitation, or other equivalent procedure based on a finding that the person has been rehabilitated,

and the person has not been convicted of a later crime punishable by death or by imprisonment for more than one year; or

(2) the conviction has been the subject of a pardon, annulment, or other equivalent procedure based on a finding of innocence.

(d) **Juvenile Adjudications.** Evidence of a juvenile adjudication is admissible under this rule only if:

(1) it is offered in a criminal case;

(2) the adjudication was of a witness other than the defendant;

(3) an adult's conviction for that offense would be admissible to attack the adult's credibility; and

(4) admitting the evidence is necessary to fairly determine guilt or innocence.

(e) **Pendency of an Appeal.** A conviction that satisfies this rule is admissible even if an appeal is pending. Evidence of the pendency is also admissible.

Rule 610. Religious Beliefs or Opinions

Evidence of a witness's religious beliefs or opinions is not admissible to attack or support the witness's credibility.

Rule 611. Mode and Order of Examining Witnesses and Presenting Evidence

(a) **Control by the Court; Purposes.** The court should exercise reasonable control over the mode and order of examining witnesses and presenting evidence so as to:

    (1)   make those procedures effective for determining the truth;

    (2)   avoid wasting time; and

    (3)   protect witnesses from harassment or undue embarrassment.

(b) **Scope of Cross-Examination.** Cross-examination should not go beyond the subject matter of the direct examination and matters affecting the witness's credibility. The court may allow inquiry into additional matters as if on direct examination.

(c) **Leading Questions.** Leading questions should not be used on direct examination except as necessary to develop the witness's testimony. Ordinarily, the court should allow leading questions:

    (1)   on cross-examination; and

    (2)   when a party calls a hostile witness, an adverse party, or a witness identified with an adverse party.

Rule 612. **Writing Used to Refresh a Witness's Memory**

(a) **Scope.** This rule gives an adverse party certain options when a witness uses a writing to refresh memory:

    (1) while testifying; or

    (2) before testifying, if the court decides that justice requires the party to have those options.

(b) **Adverse Party's Options; Deleting Unrelated Matter.** Unless 18 U.S.C. § 3500 provides otherwise in a criminal case, an adverse party is entitled to have the writing produced at the hearing, to inspect it, to cross-examine the witness about it, and to introduce in evidence any portion that relates to the witness's testimony. If the producing party claims that the writing includes unrelated matter, the court must examine the writing in camera, delete any unrelated portion, and order that the rest be delivered to the adverse party. Any portion deleted over objection must be preserved for the record.

(c) **Failure to Produce or Deliver the Writing.** If a writing is not produced or is not delivered as ordered, the court may issue any appropriate order. But if the prosecution does not comply in a criminal case, the court must strike the witness's testimony or—if justice so requires—declare a mistrial.

Rule 613.   Witness's Prior Statement

(a)   **Showing or Disclosing the Statement During Examination.** When examining a witness about the witness's prior statement, a party need not show it or disclose its contents to the witness. But the party must, on request, show it or disclose its contents to an adverse party's attorney.

(b)   **Extrinsic Evidence of a Prior Inconsistent Statement.** Extrinsic evidence of a witness's prior inconsistent statement is admissible only if the witness is given an opportunity to explain or deny the statement and an adverse party is given an opportunity to examine the witness about it, or if justice so requires. This subdivision (b) does not apply to an opposing party's statement under Rule 801(d)(2).

Rule 614.   Court's Calling or Examining a Witness

(a)   **Calling.** The court may call a witness on its own or at a party's request. Each party is entitled to cross-examine the witness.

(b)   **Examining.** The court may examine a witness regardless of who calls the witness.

(c)   **Objections.** A party may object to the court's calling or examining a witness either at that time or at the next opportunity when the jury is not present.

Rule 615. Excluding Witnesses

At a party's request, the court must order witnesses excluded so that they cannot hear other witnesses' testimony. Or the court may do so on its own. But this rule does not authorize excluding:

(a) a party who is a natural person;

(b) an officer or employee of a party that is not a natural person, after being designated as the party's representative by its attorney;

(d) a person whose presence a party shows to be essential to presenting the party's claim or defense; or

(d) a person authorized by statute to be present.

ARTICLE VII—OPINIONS AND EXPERT TESTIMONY

Rule 701. Opinion Testimony by Lay Witnesses

If a witness is not testifying as an expert, testimony in the form of an opinion is limited to one that is:

(a) rationally based on the witness's perception;

(b) helpful to clearly understanding the witness's testimony or to determining a fact in issue; and

(c) not based on scientific, technical, or other specialized knowledge within the scope of Rule 702.

Rule 702.   Testimony by Expert Witnesses

A witness who is qualified as an expert by knowledge, skill, experience, training, or education may testify in the form of an opinion or otherwise if:

(a)   the expert's scientific, technical, or other specialized knowledge will help the trier of fact to understand the evidence or to determine a fact in issue;

(b)   the testimony is based on sufficient facts or data;

(c)   the testimony is the product of reliable principles and methods; and

(d)   the expert has reliably applied the principles and methods to the facts of the case.

Rule 703.   Bases of an Expert's Opinion Testimony

An expert may base an opinion on facts or data in the case that the expert has been made aware of or personally observed. If experts in the particular field would reasonably rely on those kinds of facts or data in forming an opinion on the subject, they need not be admissible for the opinion to be admitted. But if the facts or data would otherwise be inadmissible, the proponent of the opinion may disclose them to the jury only if their probative value in helping the jury evaluate the opinion substantially outweighs their prejudicial effect.

Rule 704. **Opinion on an Ultimate Issue**

(a) **In General—Not Automatically Objectionable.** An opinion is not objectionable just because it embraces an ultimate issue.

(b) **Exception.** In a criminal case, an expert witness must not state an opinion about whether the defendant did or did not have a mental state or condition that constitutes an element of the crime charged or of a defense. Those matters are for the trier of fact alone.

Rule 705. **Disclosing the Facts or Data Underlying an Expert's Opinion**

Unless the court orders otherwise, an expert may state an opinion—and give the reasons for it—without first testifying to the underlying facts or data. But the expert may be required to disclose those facts or data on cross-examination.

Rule 706. **Court-Appointed Expert Witnesses**

(a) **Appointment Process.** On a party's motion or on its own, the court may order the parties to show cause why expert witnesses should not be appointed and may ask the parties to submit nominations. The court may appoint any expert that the parties agree on and any of its own choosing. But the court may only appoint someone who consents to act.

(b) **Expert's Role.** The court must inform the expert of the expert's duties. The court may do so in writing have a copy filed with the clerk or may do so orally at a conference in which the parties have an opportunity to participate. The expert:

(1)   must advise the parties of any findings the expert makes;

(2)   may be deposed by any party;

(3)   may be called to testify by the court or any party; and

(4)   may be cross-examined by any party, including the party that called the expert.

(c)   **Compensation.** The expert is entitled to a reasonable compensation, as set by the court. The compensation is payable as follows:

(1)   in a criminal case or in a civil case involving just compensation under the Fifth Amendment, from any funds that are provided by law; and

(2)   in any other civil case, by the parties in the proportion and at the time that the court directs—and the compensation is then charged like other costs.

(d)   **Disclosing the Appointment to the Jury.** The court may authorize disclosure to the jury that the court appointed the expert.

(e)   **Parties' Choice of Their Own Experts.** This rule does not limit a party in calling its own experts.

ARTICLE VIII—HEARSAY

Rule 801.   Definitions That Apply to This Article; Exclusions from Hearsay

(a)   **Statement.** "Statement" means a person's oral assertion, written assertion, or nonverbal conduct, if the person intended it as an assertion.

(b)   **Declarant.** "Declarant" means the person who made the statement.

(c)   **Hearsay.** "Hearsay" means a statement that:

(1)   the declarant does not make while testifying at the current trial or hearing; and

(2)   a party offers in evidence to prove the truth of the matter asserted in the statement.

(d)   **Statements That Are Not Hearsay.** A statement that meets the following conditions is not hearsay:

(1)   *A Declarant-Witness's Prior Statement.* The declarant testifies and is subject to cross-examination about a prior statement, and the statement:

(A)   is inconsistent with the declarant's testimony and was given under penalty of perjury at a trial, hearing, or other proceeding or in a deposition;

(B)   is consistent with the declarant's testimony and is offered:

          (i)   to rebut an express or implied charge that the declarant recently fabricated it or acted from a recent improper influence or motive in so testifying; or

          (ii)   to rehabilitate the declarant's credibility as a witness when attacked on another ground; or

    (C)   identifies a person as someone the declarant perceived earlier.

(2)   ***An Opposing Party's Statement.*** The statement is offered against an opposing party and:

    (A)   was made by the party in an individual or representative capacity;

    (B)   is one the party manifested that it adopted or believed to be true;

    (C)   was made by a person whom the party authorized to make a statement on the subject;

    (D)   was made by the party's agent or employee on a matter within the scope of that relationship and while it existed; or

    (E)   was made by the party's coconspirator during and in furtherance of the conspiracy.

The statement must be considered but does not by itself establish the declarant's authority

---

under (C); the existence or scope of the relationship under (D); or the existence of the conspiracy or participation in it under (E).

Rule 802. The Rule Against Hearsay

Hearsay is not admissible unless any of the following provides otherwise:

- a federal statute;
- these rules; or
- other rules prescribed by the Supreme Court.

Rule 803. Exceptions to the Rule Against Hearsay—Regardless of Whether the Declarant Is Available as a Witness

The following are not excluded by the rule against hearsay, regardless of whether the declarant is available as a witness:

(1) *Present Sense Impression.* A statement describing or explaining an event or condition, made while or immediately after the declarant perceived it.

(2) *Excited Utterance.* A statement relating to a startling event or condition, made while the declarant was under the stress of excitement that it caused.

(3) *Then-Existing Mental, Emotional, or Physical Condition.* A statement of the declarant's then-existing state of mind (such as motive,

intent, or plan) or emotional, sensory, or physical condition (such as mental feeling, pain, or bodily health), but not including a statement of memory or belief to prove the fact remembered or believed unless it relates to the validity or terms of the declarant's will.

(4) ***Statement Made for Medical Diagnosis or Treatment.*** A statement that:

   (A) is made for—and is reasonably pertinent to—medical diagnosis or treatment; and

   (B) describes medical history; past or present symptoms or sensations; their inception; or their general cause.

(5) ***Recorded Recollection.*** A record that:

   (A) is on a matter the witness once knew about but now cannot recall well enough to testify fully and accurately;

   (B) was made or adopted by the witness when the matter was fresh in the witness's memory; and

   (C) accurately reflects the witness's knowledge.

If admitted, the record may be read into evidence but may be received as an exhibit only if offered by an adverse party.

(6) *Records of a Regularly Conducted Activity.* A record of an act, event, condition, opinion, or diagnosis if:

(A) the record was made at or near the time by—or from information transmitted by—someone with knowledge;

(B) the record was kept in the course of a regularly conducted activity of a business, organization, occupation, or calling, whether or not for profit;

(C) making the record was a regular practice of that activity;

(D) all these conditions are shown by the testimony of the custodian or another qualified witness, or by a certification that complies with Rule 902(11) or (12) or with a statute permitting certification; and

(E) the opponent does not show that the source of information or the method or circumstances of preparation indicate a lack of trustworthiness.

(7) *Absence of a Record of a Regularly Conducted Activity.* Evidence that a matter is not included in a record described in paragraph (6) if:

(A) the evidence is admitted to prove that the matter did not occur or exist;

      (B)   a record was regularly kept for a matter of that kind; and

      (C)   the opponent does not show that the possible source of the information or other circumstances indicate a lack of trustworthiness.

(8)   *Public Records.* A record or statement of a public office if:

      (A)   it sets out:

           (i)   the office's activities;

           (ii)   a matter observed while under a legal duty to report, but not including, in a criminal case, a matter observed by law-enforcement personnel; or

           (iii)   in a civil case or against the government in a criminal case, factual findings from a legally authorized investigation; and

      (B)   the opponent does not show that the source of information or other circumstances indicate a lack of trustworthiness.

(9)   *Public Records of Vital Statistics.* A record of a birth, death, or marriage, if reported to a public office in accordance with a legal duty.

---

(10) *Absence of a Public Record.* Testimony—or a certification under Rule 902—that a diligent search failed to disclose a public record or statement if:

    (A) the testimony or certification is admitted to prove that

        (i) the record or statement does not exist; or

        (ii) a matter did not occur or exist, if a public office regularly kept a record or statement for a matter of that kind; and

    (B) in a criminal case, a prosecutor who intends to offer a certificate provides written notice of that intent at least 14 days before trial, and the defendant does not object in writing within 7 days of receiving the notice—unless the court sets a different time for the notice or the objection.

(11) *Records of Religious Organizations Concerning Personal or Family History.* A statement of birth, legitimacy, ancestry, marriage, divorce, death, relationship by blood or marriage, or similar facts of personal or family history, contained in a regularly kept record of a religious organization.

---

(12) *Certificates of Marriage, Baptism, and Similar Ceremonies.* A statement of fact contained in a certificate:

    (A) made by a person who is authorized by a religious organization or by law to perform the act certified;

    (B) attesting that the person performed a marriage or similar ceremony or administered a sacrament; and

    (C) purporting to have been issued at the time of the act or within a reasonable time after it.

(13) *Family Records.* A statement of fact about personal or family history contained in a family record, such as a Bible, genealogy, chart, engraving on a ring, inscription on a portrait, or engraving on an urn or burial marker.

(14) *Records of Documents That Affect an Interest in Property.* The record of a document that purports to establish or affect an interest in property if:

    (A) the record is admitted to prove the content of the original recorded document, along with its signing and its delivery by each person who purports to have signed it;

    (B) the record is kept in a public office; and

(C) a statute authorizes recording documents of that kind in that office.

(15) *Statements in Documents That Affect an Interest in Property.* A statement contained in a document that purports to establish or affect an interest in property if the matter stated was relevant to the document's purpose—unless later dealings with the property are inconsistent with the truth of the statement or the purport of the document.

(16) *Statements in Ancient Documents.* A statement in a document that was prepared before January 1, 1998, and whose authenticity is established.

(17) *Market Reports and Similar Commercial Publications.* Market quotations, lists, directories, or other compilations that are generally relied on by the public or by persons in particular occupations.

(18) *Statements in Learned Treatises, Periodicals, or Pamphlets.* A statement contained in a treatise, periodical, or pamphlet if:

(A) the statement is called to the attention of an expert witness on cross-examination or relied on by the expert on direct examination; and

(B) the publication is established as a reliable authority by the expert's admission or testimony, by another expert's testimony, or by judicial notice.

If admitted, the statement may be read into evidence but not received as an exhibit.

(19) ***Reputation Concerning Personal or Family History.*** A reputation among a person's family by blood, adoption, or marriage—or among a person's associates or in the community— concerning the person's birth, adoption, legitimacy, ancestry, marriage, divorce, death, relationship by blood, adoption, or marriage, or similar facts of personal or family history.

(20) ***Reputation Concerning Boundaries or General History.*** A reputation in a community— arising before the controversy—concerning boundaries of land in the community or customs that affect the land, or concerning general historical events important to that community, state, or nation.

(21) ***Reputation Concerning Character.*** A reputation among a person's associates or in the community concerning the person's character.

(22) ***Judgment of a Previous Conviction.*** Evidence of a final judgment of conviction if:

    (A) the judgment was entered after a trial or guilty plea, but not a nolo contendere plea;

      (B)   the conviction was for a crime punishable by death or by imprisonment for more than a year;

      (C)   the evidence is admitted to prove any fact essential to the judgment; and

      (D)   when offered by the prosecutor in a criminal case for a purpose other than impeachment, the judgment was against the defendant.

      The pendency of an appeal may be shown but does not affect admissibility.

(23)   ***Judgments Involving Personal, Family, or General History, or a Boundary.*** A judgment that is admitted to prove a matter of personal, family, or general history, or boundaries, if the matter:

      (A)   was essential to the judgment; and

      (B)   could be proved by evidence of reputation.

(24)   [*Other Exceptions.*] [Transferred to Rule 807.]

Rule 804.   **Exceptions to the Rule Against Hearsay— When the Declarant Is Unavailable as a Witness**

(a)   **Criteria for Being Unavailable.** A declarant is considered to be unavailable as a witness if the declarant:

(1)   is exempted from testifying about the subject matter of the declarant's statement because the court rules that a privilege applies;

(2)   refuses to testify about the subject matter despite a court order to do so;

(3)   testifies to not remembering the subject matter;

(4)   cannot be present or testify at the trial or hearing because of death or a then-existing infirmity, physical illness, or mental illness; or

(5)   is absent from the trial or hearing and the statement's proponent has not been able, by process or other reasonable means, to procure:

   (A)   the declarant's attendance, in the case of a hearsay exception under Rule 804(b)(1) or (6); or

   (B)   the declarant's attendance or testimony, in the case of a hearsay exception under Rule 804(b)(2), (3), or (4).

But this subdivision (a) does not apply if the statement's proponent procured or wrongfully caused the declarant's unavailability as a witness in order to prevent the declarant from attending or testifying.

(b)   **The Exceptions.** The following are not excluded by the rule against hearsay if the declarant is unavailable as a witness:

(1)   *Former Testimony.* Testimony that:

(A) was given as a witness at a trial, hearing, or lawful deposition, whether given during the current proceeding or a different one; and

(B) is now offered against a party who had—or, in a civil case, whose predecessor in interest had—an opportunity and similar motive to develop it by direct, cross-, or redirect examination.

(2) *Statement Under the Belief of Imminent Death.* In a prosecution for homicide or in a civil case, a statement that the declarant, while believing the declarant's death to be imminent, made about its cause or circumstances.

(3) *Statement Against Interest.* A statement that:

(A) a reasonable person in the declarant's position would have made only if the person believed it to be true because, when made, it was so contrary to the declarant's proprietary or pecuniary interest or had so great a tendency to invalidate the declarant's claim against someone else or to expose the declarant to civil or criminal liability; and

(B) is supported by corroborating circumstances that clearly indicate its trustworthiness, if it is offered in a criminal case as one that tends to expose the declarant to criminal liability.

(4) *Statement of Personal or Family History.* A statement about:

    (A) the declarant's own birth, adoption, legitimacy, ancestry, marriage, divorce, relationship by blood, adoption, or marriage, or similar facts of personal or family history, even though the declarant had no way of acquiring personal knowledge about that fact; or

    (B) another person concerning any of these facts, as well as death, if the declarant was related to the person by blood, adoption, or marriage or was so intimately associated with the person's family that the declarant's information is likely to be accurate.

(5) [*Other Exceptions.*] [Transferred to Rule 807.]

(6) *Statement Offered Against a Party That Wrongfully Caused the Declarant's Unavailability.* A statement offered against a party that wrongfully caused—or acquiesced in wrongfully causing—the declarant's unavailability as a witness, and did so intending that result.

Rule 805.   Hearsay Within Hearsay

Hearsay within hearsay is not excluded by the rule against hearsay if each part of the combined statements conforms with an exception to the rule.

Rule 806. Attacking and Supporting the Declarant's Credibility

When a hearsay statement—or a statement described in Rule 801(d)(2)(C), (D), or (E)—has been admitted in evidence, the declarant's credibility may be attacked, and then supported, by any evidence that would be admissible for those purposes if the declarant had testified as a witness. The court may admit evidence of the declarant's inconsistent statement or conduct, regardless of when it occurred or whether the declarant had an opportunity to explain or deny it. If the party against whom the statement was admitted calls the declarant as a witness, the party may examine the declarant on the statement as if on cross-examination.

Rule 807. Residual Exception

(a)   **In General.** Under the following circumstances, a hearsay statement is not excluded by the rule against hearsay even if the statement is not specifically covered by a hearsay exception in Rule 803 or 804:

(1)   the statement has equivalent circumstantial guarantees of trustworthiness;

(2)   it is offered as evidence of a material fact;

(3)   it is more probative on the point for which it is offered than any other evidence that the proponent can obtain through reasonable efforts; and

(4)   admitting it will best serve the purposes of these rules and the interests of justice.

(b) **Notice.** The statement is admissible only if, before the trial or hearing, the proponent gives an adverse party reasonable notice of the intent to offer the statement and its particulars, including the declarant's name and address, so that the party has a fair opportunity to meet it.

ARTICLE IX—AUTHENTICATION AND IDENTIFICATION

Rule 901. Authenticating or Identifying Evidence

(a) **In General.** To satisfy the requirement of authenticating or identifying an item of evidence, the proponent must produce evidence sufficient to support a finding that the item is what the proponent claims it is.

(b) **Examples.** The following are examples only— not a complete list—of evidence that satisfies the requirement:

    (1) *Testimony of a Witness with Knowledge.* Testimony that an item is what it is claimed to be.

    (2) *Nonexpert Opinion About Handwriting.* A nonexpert's opinion that handwriting is genuine, based on a familiarity with it that was not acquired for the current litigation.

    (3) *Comparison by an Expert Witness or the Trier of Fact.* A comparison with an authenticated specimen by an expert witness or the trier of fact.

---

(4)   ***Distinctive Characteristics and the Like.*** The appearance, contents, substance, internal patterns, or other distinctive characteristics of the item, taken together with all the circumstances.

(5)   ***Opinion About a Voice.*** An opinion identifying a person's voice—whether heard firsthand or through mechanical or electronic transmission or recording—based on hearing the voice at any time under circumstances that connect it with the alleged speaker.

(6)   ***Evidence About a Telephone Conversation.*** For a telephone conversation, evidence that a call was made to the number assigned at the time to:

(A)   a particular person, if circumstances, including self-identification, show that the person answering was the one called; or

(B)   a particular business, if the call was made to a business and the call related to business reasonably transacted over the telephone.

(7)   ***Evidence About Public Records.*** Evidence that:

(A)   a document was recorded or filed in a public office as authorized by law; or

(B)   a purported public record or statement is from the office where items of this kind are kept.

(8) ***Evidence About Ancient Documents or Data Compilations.*** For a document or data compilation, evidence that it:

 (A) is in a condition that creates no suspicion about its authenticity;

 (B) was in a place where, if authentic, it would likely be; and

 (C) is at least 20 years old when offered.

(9) ***Evidence About a Process or System.*** Evidence describing a process or system and showing that it produces an accurate result.

(10) ***Methods Provided by a Statute or Rule.*** Any method of authentication or identification allowed by a federal statute or a rule prescribed by the Supreme Court.

Rule 902. Evidence That Is Self-Authenticating

The following items of evidence are self-authenticating; they require no extrinsic evidence of authenticity in order to be admitted:

(1) ***Domestic Public Documents That Are Sealed and Signed.*** A document that bears:

 (A) a seal purporting to be that of the United States; any state, district, commonwealth, territory, or insular possession of the United States; the former Panama Canal Zone; the Trust Territory of the Pacific Islands; a political subdivision of any of these entities; or a department, agency, or officer of any entity named above; and

(B) a signature purporting to be an execution or attestation.

(2) ***Domestic Public Documents That Are Not Sealed but Are Signed and Certified.*** A document that bears no seal if:

(A) it bears the signature of an officer or employee of an entity named in Rule 902(1)(A); and

(B) another public officer who has a seal and official duties within that same entity certifies under seal—or its equivalent—that the signer has the official capacity and that the signature is genuine.

(3) ***Foreign Public Documents.*** A document that purports to be signed or attested by a person who is authorized by a foreign country's law to do so. The document must be accompanied by a final certification that certifies the genuineness of the signature and official position of the signer or attester—or of any foreign official whose certificate of genuineness relates to the signature or attestation or is in a chain of certificates of genuineness relating to the signature or attestation. The certification may be made by a secretary of a United States

embassy or legation; by a consul general, vice consul, or consular agent of the United States; or by a diplomatic or consular official of the foreign country assigned or accredited to the United States. If all parties have been given a reasonable opportunity to investigate the document's authenticity and accuracy, the court may, for good cause, either:

(A)   order that it be treated as presumptively authentic without final certification; or

(B)   allow it to be evidenced by an attested summary with or without final certification.

(4)   ***Certified Copies of Public Records.*** A copy of an official record—or a copy of a document that was recorded or filed in a public office as authorized by law—if the copy is certified as correct by:

(A)   the custodian or another person authorized to make the certification; or

(B)   a certificate that complies with Rule 902(1), (2), or (3), a federal statute, or a rule prescribed by the Supreme Court.

(5)   ***Official Publications.*** A book, pamphlet, or other publication purporting to be issued by a public authority.

(6) *Newspapers and Periodicals.* Printed material purporting to be a newspaper or periodical.

(7) *Trade Inscriptions and the Like.* An inscription, sign, tag, or label purporting to have been affixed in the course of business and indicating origin, ownership, or control.

(8) *Acknowledged Documents.* A document accompanied by a certificate of acknowledgment that is lawfully executed by a notary public or another officer who is authorized to take acknowledgments.

(9) *Commercial Paper and Related Documents.* Commercial paper, a signature on it, and related documents, to the extent allowed by general commercial law.

(10) *Presumptions Under a Federal Statute.* A signature, document, or anything else that a federal statute declares to be presumptively or prima facie genuine or authentic.

(11) *Certified Domestic Records of a Regularly Conducted Activity.* The original or a copy of a domestic record that meets the requirements of Rule 803(6)(A)–(C), as shown by a certification of the custodian or another qualified person that complies with a federal statute or a rule prescribed by the Supreme Court. Before the trial or hearing, the proponent must give an adverse party reasonable written

notice of the intent to offer the record—and must make the record and certification available for inspection—so that the party has a fair opportunity to challenge them.

(12) *Certified Foreign Records of a Regularly Conducted Activity.* In a civil case, the original or a copy of a foreign record that meets the requirements of Rule 902(11), modified as follows: the certification, rather than complying with a federal statute or Supreme Court rule, must be signed in a manner that, if falsely made, would subject the maker to a criminal penalty in the country where the certification is signed. The proponent must also meet the notice requirements of Rule 902(11).

(13) *Certified Records Generated by an Electronic Process or System.* A record generated by an electronic process or system that produces an accurate result, as shown by a certification of a qualified person that complies with the certification requirements of Rule 902(11) or (12). The proponent must also meet the notice requirements of Rule 902(11).

(14) *Certified Data Copied from an Electronic Device, Storage Medium, or File.* Data copied from an electronic device, storage medium, or file, if authenticated by a process of digital identification, as shown by a certification of a qualified person that complies with the

certification requirements of Rule 902(11) or (12). The proponent also must meet the notice requirements of Rule 902(11).

Rule 903.   Subscribing Witness's Testimony

A subscribing witness's testimony is necessary to authenticate a writing only if required by the law of the jurisdiction that governs its validity.

ARTICLE X—CONTENTS OF WRITINGS, RECORDINGS, AND PHOTOGRAPHS

Rule 1001.   Definitions That Apply to This Article

In this article:

(a)   A "writing" consists of letters, words, numbers, or their equivalent set down in any form.

(b)   A "recording" consists of letters, words, numbers, or their equivalent recorded in any manner.

(c)   A "photograph" means a photographic image or its equivalent stored in any form.

(d)   An "original" of a writing or recording means the writing or recording itself or any counterpart intended to have the same effect by the person who executed or issued it. For electronically stored information, "original" means any printout—or other output readable by sight—if it accurately reflects the information. An "original" of a photograph includes the negative or a print from it.

(e) A "duplicate" means a counterpart produced by a mechanical, photographic, chemical, electronic, or other equivalent process or technique that accurately reproduces the original.

Rule 1002.　Requirement of the Original

An original writing, recording, or photograph is required in order to prove its content unless these rules or a federal statute provides otherwise.

Rule 1003.　Admissibility of Duplicates

A duplicate is admissible to the same extent as the original unless a genuine question is raised about the original's authenticity or the circumstances make it unfair to admit the duplicate.

Rule 1004.　Admissibility of Other Evidence of Content

An original is not required and other evidence of the content of a writing, recording, or photograph is admissible if:

(a) all the originals are lost or destroyed, and not by the proponent acting in bad faith;

(b) an original cannot be obtained by any available judicial process;

(c) the party against whom the original would be offered had control of the original; was at that time put on notice, by pleadings or otherwise, that the original would be a subject of proof at the trial or hearing; and fails to produce it at the trial or hearing; or

(d)　　the writing, recording, or photograph is not closely related to a controlling issue.

Rule 1005.　Copies of Public Records to Prove Content

The proponent may use a copy to prove the content of an official record—or of a document that was recorded or filed in a public office as authorized by law—if these conditions are met: the record or document is otherwise admissible; and the copy is certified as correct in accordance with Rule 902(4) or is testified to be correct by a witness who has compared it with the original. If no such copy can be obtained by reasonable diligence, then the proponent may use other evidence to prove the content.

Rule 1006.　Summaries to Prove Content

The proponent may use a summary, chart, or calculation to prove the content of voluminous writings, recordings, or photographs that cannot be conveniently examined in court. The proponent must make the originals or duplicates available for examination or copying, or both, by other parties at a reasonable time and place. And the court may order the proponent to produce them in court.

Rule 1007.　Testimony or Statement of a Party to Prove Content

The proponent may prove the content of a writing, recording, or photograph by the testimony, deposition, or written statement of the party against whom the evidence is offered. The proponent need not account for the original.

Rule 1008. Functions of the Court and Jury

Ordinarily, the court determines whether the proponent has fulfilled the factual conditions for admitting other evidence of the content of a writing, recording, or photograph under Rule 1004 or 1005. But in a jury trial, the jury determines—in accordance with Rule 104(b)—any issue about whether:

(a)   an asserted writing, recording, or photograph ever existed;

(b)   another one produced at the trial or hearing is the original; or

(c)   other evidence of content accurately reflects the content.

Article XI—Miscellaneous Rules

Rule 1101. Applicability of the Rules

(a)   **To Courts and Judges.** These rules apply to proceedings before:

* United States district courts;

* United States bankruptcy and magistrate judges;

* United States courts of appeals;

* the United States Court of Federal Claims; and

- the district courts of Guam, the Virgin Islands, and the Northern Mariana Islands.

(b) **To Cases and Proceedings.** These rules apply in:

- civil cases and proceedings, including bankruptcy, admiralty, and maritime cases;

- criminal cases and proceedings; and

- contempt proceedings, except those in which the court may act summarily.

(c) **Rules on Privilege.** The rules on privilege apply to all stages of a case or proceeding.

(d) **Exceptions.** These rules—except for those on privilege—do not apply to the following:

(1) the court's determination, under Rule 104(a), on a preliminary question of fact governing admissibility;

(2) grand-jury proceedings; and

(3) miscellaneous proceedings such as:

- extradition or rendition;

- issuing an arrest warrant, criminal summons, or search warrant;

- a preliminary examination in a criminal case;

- sentencing;

- granting or revoking probation or supervised release; and

- • considering whether to release on bail or otherwise.

(e) **Other Statutes and Rules.** A federal statute or a rule prescribed by the Supreme Court may provide for admitting or excluding evidence independently from these rules.

Rule 1102. Amendments

These rules may be amended as provided in 28 U.S.C. § 2072.

Rule 1103. Title

These rules may be cited as the Federal Rules of Evidence.